About the Author

Iain McIntosh was a nurse in the embryonic National Health Service before graduating as a doctor from Edinburgh University. He became a family physician and served in a rural and urban general practice partnership for over thirty years. His experiences and the vagaries of human life provide the anecdotes nad tales recounted within this book. His working life encompassed the early days of the developing NHS and paternalistic, holistic, general medical practice, which may prove to have been the zenith of high quality, UK patient community care.

He published his first article when aged eighteen and continued writing thereafter, publishing both professional and general books. A long interest in travel and medicine brought professional recognition and award of FFTMRCPS (Glas). His long writing and medical career owes much of its success to the unstinting support of a wife who played an integral part in the medical practice.

http://www.fast-print.net/bookshop

First published by Fast-Print Publishing of Peterborough, England, 2016

Copyright

ISBN 978 1 7845 6422 3

Acknowledgements

The author wishes to thank his wife and daughter for their support and encouragement in writing this book. Acknowledgement is made of the latter's help in proof–reading and her courage, fortitude, steadfastness and consideration for others in a time of great personal adversity.

Chris and his wife, very good friends, provided valuable input and wise suggestions with proof-reading and their assistance was much appreciated.

Thanks also to Gordon of Monument Press for help in creation of the cover and lay-out in the production of the book.

Although a life's experience and observations of patients' personalities and behaviour has been drawn upon in creating contents of the novel, the characters and locations involved are entirely fictitious and a product of the author's imagination. Any resemblance to real persons alive or dead is purely coincidental. Comments about primary care practice are however relevant to the time and the early days of the innovative NHS.

Preface

"Allan Welman, pay attention! Take a good look at the High School building when you pass it, for you will never see the inside," thundered out Mr. Hardman my primary school teacher. A soulless bachelor broad in girth and limb, he disciplined his charges by frequent strapping of a leather belt on outstretched hands. A recalcitrant pupil, I became familiar with its painful application and recall the misery of being belted nine times in one day for alleged misconduct. Forceful persuasion however perhaps encouraged learning.

Accepting his unsolicited prediction, my entry examination pass to St Jude's High School was a surprise. An indifferent pupil, I left the institution in 1949, before I was fifteen, to become an apprentice dental mechanic. The drudgery of fabricating dentures for an edentulous public intent on acquiring free artificial teeth, brought belated appreciation of the value of education in advancement. The infant National Health service encouraged academic achievement. I changed direction to become a ward orderly. Working with staff in St. Jude's Infirmary, I was encouraged to enrol in further education evening classes and acquire higher educational certificates. Then came the inevitable "call to the colours".

After World War Two, compulsory military service continued with the conscription of young men, which ensured that most eighteen-year old youths would spend two unwilling years serving Queen and Country in various roles. After Royal Air Force enrollment, drilling and training courses, I was posted to the Middle East Air Force to serve in Libya and Egypt as a nurse in the Medical branch. The experience was life-changing and I determined to become a family doctor on demobilisation.

Six grinding years at Edinburgh University provided basic medical education culminating in acquisition of the coveted MB.Ch.B degree. A further two years hard graft as a Hospital House Officer in the infant National Health Service, paved the way for a career as a general medical practitioner and the potential to work in hospital speciality practice.

At that time family doctoring was very different from the community patient-care practised today. Medications and investigations were limited and support services in short supply. Rickets, poliomyelitis, scarlet fever, tuberculosis (TB) and smallpox stalked the land and killed, or invalided, sufferers. Common acute infections such as tonsillitis, whooping cough, measles and erysipelas could fell young victims and quickly become life-threatening. Antibiotic treatment was limited to sulphonamides, tetracyclines and basic penicillin, the latter primarily given by injection. Skin-stitching, lancing boils, excising lumps, syringing ears, bandaging and plastering was part of standard GP. practice. This also involved the tedious manual sterilising of equipment before the arrival of the pre-disposable package era.

Personal accident and mishap brought many consultations, for there was much personal trauma in the home and at work. First-aid was sought from the local doctor, not hospital Accident and Emergency Departments. Sources were open fires, gas-lights and appliances at home. At work, in the absence of health and safety regulations, many dangerous industrial practices existed. Treatment of heart and chest conditions involved often ineffectual medicines and potions, which ensured chronicity and premature death. Unshielded X-ray equipment was used for screening, creating unforeseen health hazards. Child-birth, was still accompanied by high foetal mortality rates and long term maternal morbidity.

There was scant social and professional interaction between medical partners, who had amalgamated to share on-call commitments and maximise income. Junior partners worked long anti-social hours for a pittance and waited up to fifteen years to become a principal and reach income parity. Wives acted as unpaid receptionists and telephone message-takers.

The doctor's office-the Surgery-was often an integral part of the family home. Non-appointment consultations ran from 9am. until 7 or 8pm. mid-week and on Saturday mornings, with one doctor covering out-of-hours emergencies. Patients waited until seen, but were never turned away and surgeries ran till the last patient presented late in the evening. The consultation could be a brief few minutes, for those seeking a sickness certificate, or a prolonged half-hour medical examination.

"Hands on" clinical practice was standard and encouraged. Many manual procedures now carried out in hospital casualty departments were performed, from wound-stitching to minor operations under local or general anaesthetic. With passing years, fewer surgical procedures took place and general practitioners lost much of their manual dexterity, as they performed fewer clinical procedures. General practice doctors were predominantly male. Hospital contracts, domiciliary obstetrics and house visits ensured busy practice and long working days.

The medical ethos of the time determined that the GP managed the patient to the limit of acquired skill and only referred on to the hospital when additional investigation and clinical expertise was required. The embryonic NHS initially offered free consultations, spectacles, dentures, wigs and prostheses to all and free prescriptions for many. The public responded with high demand for new services. Many people failed to appreciate that the right to a universal, free health service brought with it a personal responsibility not to misuse the facility. As car ownership was still only for the affluent and public bus services intermittent, the unwell often had to be visited at home. House calls occupied much of the day and disrupted many a night for the duty-doctor.

A glut of doctors returning from the armed services had swamped the GP. job market and there were few vacancies in general medical practice for newly qualified practitioners. A hundred young doctors often applied for a single vacant post. Many emigrated to Canada and Australia in search of work. I was lucky to find a post in a partnership of doctors working from an old Georgian house in Harborough, a small market town. Situated on the edge of the Lothian mine-fields in the Scottish Borders, it was the focal point of the practice area.

The four-partner practice occupied an old, poorly-adapted Victorian building and was responsible for the holistic health care of 13,000 patents every day and night of the year. The surgery milieu had one attraction - the rear windows had extensive views across the Border hills - a glimpse of which could lighten my heart and break the tedium of onerous patient consultations.

Offices, comprising two consulting rooms, waiting-room and a tiny cupboard containing thousands of records and their keeper, were housed on only one level of the three storey building. On my arrival, there were, three typewriters, three telephones and one secretary. Thirty years later, every room on all three floors was in service, an indicator of substantial change over time. Six doctors, eight clerks, practice manager, three attached nurses, practice nurse, four health visitors, social worker and part time psychologist managed 2,000 fewer patients. A telephone and word-processor lay on every desk with a plethora of supportive printers, photocopiers, scanners and filing cabinets. Progressive decades had embraced modernity. The computer had come to rule the roost.

At that time the digital age was decades away and filing shelves held A5 size envelopes stuffed with letters of every size and hue. A lined, brown card was intended to record GP. consultations. Few held complete records of appointments and many were devoid of written comment. Most practitioners carried patient's histories in memory and over time built up detailed recollections of extended families, a benefit to patients. Sharing of information between partners was more haphazard. House call messages were often written on scraps of paper and left with receptionist, chemist, or neighbour, for collection by the doctor on home visit rounds.

Patient /doctor/receptionist communication during the house-call round depended on access to the ubiquitous red, street-side telephone box, as few patients had domestic telephone service. Unusually, one of my partners had a radio telephone, which was so bulky it took up most of the rear seat of his car. The first mobile telephone to appear was greeted with great excitement for it promised emancipation for the "on-call" doctor, who need no longer remain close to landlines while "on-call". The contraption was the size of four bricks and weighed the same. First requirement on a house visit was to plug in the phone for recharging, as charge lasted only twenty minutes.

Despite the weighty demands of "on-call" commitment to patients, the majority of family doctors were committed to patient care. For many it was a vocation. Patient needs were paramount before family responsibilities. By day and night, if patient demand was genuine, their care was put before family requirements. Harassed wives coped with both family and surgery needs and The Practice dominated family life.

Much of patient demand was trivial and routine, but practitioner-personalised lists ensured continuity of care from cradle to grave and enduring patient relationships. Over time, came professional intimacy with extended families covering three generations. It was not unusual for grandchildren, mother and grandma to appear together for consultation.

There was diversity in character between urban and rural patients. Patients from the country were fiercely independent and made few demands on the practice except in emergency. Town dwellers took full advantage of open, free access to GPs and casualty units. Some of them lived in ancient tenements, in two and three room flats with cold running water and a lavatory on the landing, which might serve several flats. Large families ensured overcrowding with several children sharing a bed. A shared wash-house and drying green occupied the back court. This was the play area for the tenement's children. There was gas-lighting in the flats, a sink with wash tub, a coal-fired cooking range, and no other source of room heating. Rooms were over-warm in summer and cold, dank places in winter.

Many of the tenants were suffering from chronic bronchitis and respiratory disease, the end-result of long years working in the nations' coal- mines. These were "purple puffers and blue bloaters" hardly able to traverse a room or climb a stair, who required regular visits. Home maternity deliveries were routine with mother and baby needing home visitation. New mothers underwent a week-long post-delivery "lying-in" period. This was not clinically wise, for prompt ambulation would have decreased the likelihood of post-natal complications. It however gave the hard-pressed woman a break from the demands of immediate family care, as grandmothers and neighbours rallied round to care for other children.

In pre-contraceptive pill days, abstinence was the only certain means of family-size control. Practised in name rather than practice, many women produced new offspring with regularity and large families were normal. Snotty nosed urchins thronged the stairs and back-court play-ground, which was a constant source of infection and trauma. Many had scarred knees from gravel falls. Gentian-stained heads were testimony to the impetigo infection common in an over-crowded environ.

Many decent, hard-working young couples struggled for a livelihood in this environment. The free NHS however brought assurance that they and their children would have a healthier future than their forebears. In time, all would leave antiquated housing for the council flat, or the modest bungalow, in large impersonal building schemes. The improved amenities were appreciated, but they missed the community spirit and neighbour support provided in old dwellings.

For fifty years after the creation of the NHS. the pattern of general medical practice was sustained by a GP work-load and working hours risible by today's standards. I struggled through 250 consultations per week for fifty weeks in the year. Many were follow-up consultations, but an endless stream of people with acute and chronic illness, physical and mental disability, social problems and hypochondriasis, flowed through the surgery in an endless tide of morbidity.

Commitment, endeavour and hard work went unappreciated, until the model was destroyed by politicians. The general practitioner would become part of a team of health-workers delegating management practices and chores in a role far-divorced from early NHS days. Family doctors lost skills and restricted access in the process and people had no option but to turn to Accident and Emergency departments and beleaguered hospital resources. Patients unwittingly lost the personal awareness and immediacy of family doctor care of yester-year. History may reveal that these were the golden years of quality, holistic family practice, later decimated by politicians within and out-with the medical profession..

The accessible, paternalistic, patronising role of the family practitioner was then unquestioned and local doctors were respected by the public. The family doctor was privileged to peer into the intimacies and complexities of human behaviour and experience the best and worst of social interactions.

There were challenging and intriguing contacts with colourful personalities, conniving rogues, deceitful criminals, saints and sinners, the ill and hypochondriac. These encounters, drawn from thousands of consultations prior to retirement, enlivened the practice day and were a rich reward for long, demanding years in general medical practice. This novel dwells upon some of these entertaining, therapeutic, tragic and elevating, patient consultations and events drawn from a life's experience as a family doctor. It tells my story of bygone practice and local medical care.

"While I'm here Doctor" was often the patients' pre-amble to divulging a potentially serious health concern.

A Traumatic Baptism

It was nearing the end of a beautiful, crisp, early spring day, with hills and glens clothed in grass and bracken, of yellow and russet hue. A dying sun was casting orange-red rays over nearby summits and the deeper gullies were shadowed in blue, anticipating a cold night to come. An hour away from the welcoming fireside of home, I was driving to a routine house call, to a shepherd's croft on the edge of the practice area almost 30 miles from the surgery. It was my first introductory day as a family doctor in rural medical practice. The culmination of years of study and clinical learning, I was at peace with the world and in harmony with the surroundings.

The single-track road was narrow, winding and bordered intermittently by high hedges. It climbed up and down between streams and mini-gorges and required driving skill and concentration to traverse. Declining visibility added hazard as evening turned to night. I was enjoying the driving challenge until turning one tight corner, I almost rammed into a vehicle slewed broadside across the road. A large truck, carrying stone from a nearby quarry, had been in a collision. I could not see beyond the massive vehicle, which was leaking petrol into the roadside ditch, but a badly battered car-wheel-arch poked from under its rear wheel. Grabbing my emergency bag, I rushed round the high flank of the truck to come upon a disaster scene, morbidly displayed in the lurid light of the setting sun.

A thin-skinned Citroën 15 CV, the French "people's car" of the fifties, had been cleft almost in two on impact with the truck. Wreckage had slammed into a rock-wall at the road-side. Oil and water seeped across the road, tinged pink in the failing light, almost inseparable in colour from pools of blood turgidly flowing from two bodies lying in the debris. The open door of the truck displayed an inert driver slumped across the steering wheel. Beside the car lay the two occupants. The macabre scene seemed frozen in time, with no movement or sound from victims.

My initial intervention was over-hasty. I raced across to the nearest casualty, who was lying on his back, half over the sill of the wrecked car doorway. A leg was lying at a right angle to the body. I tried to realign both as I sought for a pulse. Lifting the trousered limb, the lower leg separated from its owner! Effectively amputated in the crash, only a sliver of skin had connected it to the patient.

Training reflexes now kicked-in and I triaged the casualties. The truck-driver had a head injury and was unconscious. A young woman had been thrown through the car wind-screen and was dead. The amputee needed immediate emergency care. He was breathing, although unresponsive to stimuli. I checked his airway was clear and quickly applied a tourniquet to the leg stump. While setting up an intravenous drip line in an arm, the distinctive engine-sound of a tractor announced its arrival, as one rumbled round the corner and braked to a sudden stop.

A startled farmer, with a cigarette dangling from his lips, gazed down at me from his high perch.

"Call an ambulance." I said forcibly. "We need immediate help," and peremptorily added, "Put out that cigarette!"

Taciturn like many of his breed, he surveyed the traumatic scene silently for a moment and then noisily shifted gears to reverse in haste up the road, at his top speed of 10 mph.

"I'll be back, "he shouted over the labouring engine and was away. In days before mobile telephones, few houses or farms owned a telephone and communication in emergency depended on access to the universal red roadside telephone box. The nearest was some miles away.

I bandaged bleeding wounds on the patient's other leg until the farmer ultimately returned. The traumatised leg had been torn roughly apart mid-thigh and the shattered femur was sticking grotesquely from the stump. Although the man had lost much blood, the main leg artery was now only oozing under the tourniquet. The vessel had been twisted tight with the torsion of the leg, which had saved him from bleeding to death. I made a huge pad of cotton wool and absorbent gauze and rammed it over the torn end of the limb fixing it in place with a rubber bandage.

"How can I help?" queried the farmer on his return and I thrust a venous drip bottle into his hands.

"Hold this upright while I see to the driver." I instructed. Gingerly, I examined the truck's occupant who regained semi-consciousness as I checked his vital signs. He muttered a few words incoherently then, returned to limited alertness. "I couldn't stop. I couldn't stop." he mumbled, then lapsed back into coma. I eased his bulky frame on to one side and along the front seat of the cab into the coma position. He was breathing stertorously, but evenly and I worried that he had suffered brain injury. There was no further emergency aid I could provide and I returned to the farmer's side.

Accustomed to animal accident and tragedy, he was stoically holding the drip bottle vertical as the fluid infusion dripped into the injured man.

"Abe Sampson." He introduced himself laconically.

"Dr. Welman", I returned.

The patient, in his early twenties, stirred and groaned and I tried to elicit more information about possible injuries. As I gently prodded his abdomen suspecting internal injury, probing fingers palpated a rigid unyielding stomach wall. Time and transport was now vital if he was to survive until reaching hospital. Meanwhile I could only treat survivors for shock, keep them immobile, warm and retaining body fluids until transportation.

"Bluidy awful." Was the only other verbal contribution made by Abe, in masterly understatement. He stood silent while the fluid dripped into the victim's veins and I pondered on what further aid was practicable.

The emergency vehicle ultimately appeared, an un-sprung, converted military ambulance fitted, with four crude, paired, horizontal patient-carriers and two-poled canvas stretchers. A pull-down wall-seat and roof-attached cupboard were the only other contents. We transferred the two men into the ambulance. Abe phlegmatically stayed at the accident scene with the corpse, after the two patients were hoisted on to stretchers and belted on to the carriers.

"I'll see to your car doc," Abe assured me phlegmatically as we set off," and I'll tell auld Jenkins at Cairnmount,"you'll no' be seein' him the day," alluding to the crofter up the road at my intended destination. He unemotionally, pulled some logs across the road to close it to further traffic, behaving as if the incident was not untoward in his daily life. Living far-distant from urban support, hill farmers were self-reliant and resilient to trauma. Personal injury and tragedy was not rare on lonely farms as I would find over coming years. Farmers, wives and children were undemonstrative, stoical and tolerant of grief and hardship, very different from the self-centred, often hysterically reacting urban population. Abe was a classic of his breed-taciturn, unemotional and undemonstrative; I would meet him regularly tending his animals over ensuing years.

The ambulance driver was unaccompanied and I perforce had to continue administrations to the patients on the way to the hospital. The drip equipment was fixed to one of the stretcher supports and I continued to care for the casualties. Incarcerated in the back of the vehicle, which swayed alarmingly on the many bends and bounced disconcertingly over humps on the road, I promptly suffered motion-sickness feeling squeamish and dizzy. To distract thoughts from imminent vomiting, I lurched to the top end of the vehicle where the roof cupboard housed emergency medications and opened it. This was another mistake for, as the ambulance swerved round a bend, the contents cascaded out and rolled around the floor. Much of the rest of a long journey was spent retrieving injectable drugs from inaccessible hiding-places as they rolled across the floor.

We finally reached the hospital and pulled into the emergency parking-bay. The rear door was immediately opened by a porter and female assistant. I had stowed the amputated leg on top of one of the upper stretchers and unnoticed, the jolts on the journey had dislodged it from under a blanket and pushed it up against the rear door. It promptly fell out at the porter's feet to his anguish and the girl's scream.

A staff nurse arrived and I briefed her as she organised patient transfer.

"They will go straight to theatre," she assured me and staff promptly sped the injured men into the trauma unit. The truck driver had blood clot removed from his skull and was left with initial memory loss, but recovered fully. The young man, George Anderson a student, was less fortunate. His stump was surgically reconstructed and blood transfusion was successful. His injured spleen was removed leaving him with lowered immunity to infection, which was life threatening when antibiotic intervention was then limited.

I was left contemplating how to return to my far distant car. A phone-call to the surgery brought fellow partner Percy to my aid. His bright red and much prized sports car screeched to a stop outside the emergency ward door and he beckoned me to join him. The car was low-slung with minuscule seating, which suited his small stature, but required awkward bodily contortions for me to board the vehicle and squeeze long legs under the dashboard. Partners referred to his pride and joy as "the phallic symbol".

Boyish, bouncing and dynamic, Percy dashed everywhere at speed. He drove the car with scant regard for speed limits and delighted in swooping round tight bends on Border roads. The return journey to retrieve my vehicle was faster and more death-threatening than the outward trip by ambulance. Was this I wondered the workaday model for my future career in practice? Fortunately these occasions were rare and routine family practice much more mundane.

George took up his studies again. He returned to the family farm residence for vacations and I would occasionally meet him on my rounds.

"I am only here thanks to you," he would say, although it was the surgeon who had saved him. He survived until graduating, when tragically; a severe infection ended his life prematurely.

The years following this traumatic incident would bring challenging medical events, dramatic social interactions and complex patient relationships but, few would surpass this dramatic introduction to rural doctoring.

Village Doctor

A few days previously the great medical adventure had begun. The over-loaded Renault 4 L car - our pride and joy - with its tubular steel bumpers and, dash-board knob-stick, gear-change, motored into the Scottish Borders. Stalled for an hour in traffic due to a road traffic accident, our worldly goods had preceded us. Evening was drawing in as we eventually reached our goal, the small village of Riverside nestling beside the boisterous river Har as it surged to the nearby sea. The village would be home to wife Ann, two toddlers and Kim a very large Labrador. I was to be the village doctor in a group practice centre established five miles away in Harborough.

We arrived in a cul-de-sac of semi-detached bungalows and instantly recognised our home. The removal van had arrived long before us and removers, tired of waiting, had dumped prized possessions on driveway and lawn of the new abode. Heavy furniture, carelessly-draped with carpets, was piled haphazardly across interior floors as workmen high-tailed back to base. Precious china and ornaments teetered on precarious shelving, in a dwelling stripped naked by departing owners. A dull, light bulb, dangling from a lone wire, poorly lit one room as darkness fell. We were marooned, with no local contacts, two distraught children and an over- excited dog. This was not the envisaged triumphal entry to our first home. We bedded down on the floor. Ensconced in one room, surrounded by abandoned packing cases and furniture, the future did not appear too bright. Plaintive wails came from older daughter Ginny,

"When are we going home mummy?" added to our plight.

Kim – an indulged pet - was however enthusiastically cavorting around, sniffing out his new quarters. He was first to announce our presence to village and neighbours. He had been accustomed to a house-bound existence and sleeping in front of the fire. I was determined he should now occupy a kennel that I had built to stand in the garden. The dog was unwillingly secured in this shelter and we prepared for a sleep, denied for the next two hours. Kim objected to his new domicile and a battle for domination ensued, as with barks of increasing crescendo and frequency, he indicated displeasure at his incarceration. Commands, scolds then exasperated whacks brought no cessation to his vocal performance.

"Quiet. Stop that racket. Shut up you brute." Orders gave way to pleading and entreaties for silence, all to no avail.

As the small hours of the morning came upon us, I considered that we might soon be expelled from the village by distraught locals. The tiresome, solidly muscled dog accentuated the noisy cacophony by physically dragging his heavy kennel round the stone-slabbed garden, creating reverberations that swelled out into the night. Finally, defeated by canine cunning and aware that a village lynching might face me in the light of day, I succumbed. At 2 am, the triumphant beast was released to exultantly join us on the floor. For months to come, as I travelled round the practice, the opening conversation was usually,

"I heard that you had arrived!"

A mad frenetic weekend followed as we brought some organisation to chaos, before I reported for work. The branch surgery was established in the best room of the local farmer's home which abutted on to the main street of the village.

Pulling into the farmyard and parking beside several horse carts and ancient tractors, I approached the grandly described Hillfoot Surgery which occupied the front and best room of the farmhouse. Farmer, Archie Greenaway was a very large, ebullient character, who discoursed in a broad Lancastrian accent unadulterated by decades of living in Scotland. He greeted me invariably with,

"What's oop doc?" lisping out the words, between battered remnants of teeth that had lost the fight against tooth decay. A few stumps guarded his palate as he smiled a welcome. His dialect and the lisp ensured that his speech, especially when excited, was often incomprehensible. He wore a battered cap, rarely off his head, and stubble on cheeks and chops, testified to rare attacks from a razor. His jacket had bulging and torn pockets. Trousers were held up over a protuberant gut with baling twine, in a losing battle to keep them waist-high.

His wife Jane was more taciturn and a lass from the Yorkshire dales, with an accent I struggled to interpret. She invariably wore a long striped, blue and white apron and Wellington boots. She was tiny and slim with a girth in inverse proportion to her husband's. They made an incongruous pair and seemed superficially, despite forty years of marriage, to have little in common. The Wars of the Roses had never been settled in their minds and they belittled each other's origins at every opportunity. A good baker she enlivened my visits with her culinary presentations.

"Time for tea before you start Doctor Welman," she would state, brooking no refusal," I have a fruit cake for you, "and a large freshly-made confection would appear for my personal consumption. She then proudly escorted me into the best room of the house which doubled as the "consulting room". It was furnished with a table and chairs and the adjacent living room stood in as a temporary waiting room. To my dismay the room did not include either examination couch or desk.

"Is there no place for the patient to lie down," I asked taken aback.

"Auld doctor didn't need it," Jane rasped in explanation. She was a chain-smoker and had the characteristic hacking cough associated with smoking addicts. She vacated her homely abode for afternoon sessions and revelled in her unofficial position as gate-keeper to the doctor - an unpaid, unsolicited status I never dared question.

Readied for consultation, I peered in to a deep wall cupboard.

"All the records are in there," Jane had pointed out, before departing for her fireside to chat with waiting patients. Cupboard shelves held discarded shoe-boxes full of brown envelopes containing faded cards, to be written-up by the doctor after each consultation, a chore which my predecessor had obviously avoided. All were in pristine condition, neatly addressed, but without detail of medical history or medication! The cupboard also held an impressive collection of unlabelled quart-size bottles holding liquids of varying colour. When the first patients presented, I requested details of their clinical history and medication. Replies to the former were sketchy. Answers to questions on medical status were illustrative and inventive but not clinically helpful,

"A patch on the lung. A whistle in my chest. A dicky heart."

However they were marginally more aware of their medications, knowing they were taking the green, blue or red bottle.

Pharmacy lectures had not prepared me for detective work and the identity of the contents eluded me. For some months, I dealt out supplies of coloured bottles with Latinised labels, until their dearth forced replenishment. Partners revealed that the liquids were mist. mag. trisil, mist.mag. trisil et tinct. carb. co., neurophospates, mist. Morph. et ipecac and variants of these, to ring changes in colour. I grew fond of these preparations, which were in much demand, for settling the bowels, easing the cough and enhancing the spirit. Mag. trisil et tinct. carb. co. became a prescribing favourite. It was good for improving flatulence and I retained it in my pharmacopoeia for many years. It was cheap, popular and successful. Tincture of carbonate compound had a deep-red, easily identifiable colour.

Evil-smelling pastes in white jars on one shelf provided the base for liniments and ointments, which were mixed on a marble slab, or concocted using a mortar and pestle. There were even moulds for making pills which I disdained, but I had to count tablets into cardboard containers - a time - wasting procedure. Metrication came in time and still I gave these traditional liquid prescriptions to patients ordered in minims and ounces. Twelve years after the demise of the old imperial measures, I noticed that one of the patient's bottles for the mixture colour was very red. By chance the next patient produced a very pale pink bottle when requested.

Joe Hall, the local chemist, was a hyperactive little fellow with a lively sense of humour. A careful dispenser who could read my almost illegible prescription scrawl with ease, I questioned him discretely about the quantities he was dispensing.

"Joe," "How much tincture do you add to the mixture?

"One drop which used to be a minim." he said authoritatively. Other local pharmacists then revealed they were adding a variable number of drops to the mixture, which dictated its colour and perhaps its potency. Regretfully, the time had come to move into the 20th century and the pink bottle became a remedy of the past.

Over time, I gradually acquired the furniture and equipment required of a modern surgery, but Hillfoot branch surgery sessions remained unconventional. Archie farmed the local acres. Stolidly-built,a local Councillor and pillar of the village community, he enjoyed vocalising in a vernacular which I gradually learned to understand.

"Na thin Doc," he would lisp embarking on a pet topic and I never failed to marvel at the remarkable assembly of broken and blackened front teeth in his dentition. After many chats with him at tea-breaks when he discoursed about his animals, I was inveigled into supporting his animal care, although it was questionably legal for a medical practitioner to treat animals. He would imperiously disturb my patient consultation,

"A needs tha'help. A needs tha' now. I need a hand wi' t'piggin" he would command, before I could call the next patient. In a nearby stall a pig giving birth to a multiplicity of off-spring would be in obstructed labour. With muttered apologies, I would desert the consultation for animal obstetrics. Kneeling in straw litter, ineffectively trying to protect trousers from soiling, I would lend a hand to clear the birth-canal, whereupon another little piglet would parachute on to the straw.

Waiting patients were remarkably accepting of these interruptions and tolerant of the dung odour emanating from my shoes and apparel on my return to formal consultations. They took a keen interest in the size of the litter."

"How many now Doctor?" or, with some ribaldry from a local worthy,

"Guid practice for the weans." "You'll be a fair hand wi' triplets!"

These interludes enlivened routine consultations with ancient villagers presenting with gout and heart problems. An emergency call would come from far across the practice, often involving a return run of sixty miles and I would apologetically leave the consulting-room on an errand of mercy. An hour or two later, it was surprising to see all the waiting patients still in place. Such patience, I marvelled. It was some time before I discovered the subterfuge.

"It's remarkable that everyone waits so patiently for my return" I remarked to Jane.

"Nowt remarkable abou' it," she retorted, "Its m' red mat."! She routinely placed a mat on the pavement outside the surgery to advise when I was in surgery, or my arrival was imminent. Patients disappeared home until the reappearance of the red mat advised that consulting was about to resume.

Jane, cigarette stuck to lower lip was sublimely unaware of her incongruous personal attire which was more appropriate to a butcher's shop. She enlivened her day by quizzing patients about their maladies, while they waited to see me. Devoted to Player's cigarettes she was usually enveloped in her personal smoke cloud. She was a good listener, had a comprehensive knowledge of villager's maladies gleaned over many years and was a repository for some secrets which they did not divulge to me. Never a malicious gossip, their confidences were safe with her. The ancient door between consulting-room and living-room creaked noisily as patients departed and this was the cue for Jane to announce loudly if wheezily through a cloud of smoke,

"Next patient please," in her assumed role, as gate-keeper to the inner sanctum.

To my discomfort she would seek to lighten my work load.

"Ye were tha' busy an' runnin' late. I jest telt auld Mrs. James to tek an extra dose of tha' bottle and see you next week." she would aver. My gentle recriminations fell on deaf ears and no harm seemed to come from her interventions. She unwittingly often provided a counselling servicc with worldly advice to her confidants.

I soon settled into the role of village doctor which had some drawbacks. When off-duty and labouring stripped to the waist, endeavouring to tame a wild garden, villagers would approach and lean across the fence in apparently friendly conversation. Their discourse was a subterfuge.

"A nice day for the garden and your day off," they would observe, then with subtlety, they would slip in prescription and diagnostic requests. The preamble was a refrain I would here frequently in practice years.

"While I am here Doctor, "then as a further subterfuge,

"To save you time Doctor, could I just have Emily's prescription," or,

"I have windy stomach pains Doc. What do you think it might be? I don't want to have to call you out later." It was difficult to retain dignity far less patience in such a situation.

Obstetric care, an important part of family practice, was very demanding. Home and hospital deliveries impinged heavily on day and night, free family time. On many occasions, with an enlarged personal clan of four small children finally dressed, car-bound and ready to set off for a day trip, an urgent call would come in. Grudgingly, I would answer the persistent telephone rings.

"Mrs.......is having her baby, the nurse needs you now."

Leaving a frustrated Ann and our little ones, I would streak off to some woman in child-birth. Often the delivery was far from imminent and by the time the head crowned and the baby was born several hours had passed. Precious time off-duty hours, had been lost to Ann's and toddlers' voluble discontent. Safe delivery of an eagerly awaited child was however a satisfying experience for me and mother and often established a lasting bond of trust between us.

Home confinements were always potentially hazardous. The birth process could go wrong with abrupt rapidity. In the days before ultrasound and uterine scans there could be an unexpected breech presentation, or presenting umbilical cord. Forceps deliveries in the home, even with the help of a skilled midwife, were always fraught with anxiety. Even after a safe delivery, retained after-births compounded my anxieties, when the attention of mother and relatives was all on the joyous reception of the new-born. Complicated child-births always seemed to occur in farm cottages far distant from the aid of the hospital-based obstetric flying squad.

Mother and child were then at high risk and foetal and maternal mortality a serious concern in hospital and GP obstetrics. An integral part of primary medical care, domestic obstetrics challenged my professional prowess and equanimity. Many of these births occurred at night and not only the "mother to be "would labour through the small hours of the morning. A successful outcome with well babe and mum was intensely satisfying, but some deliveries left psychological scars when the birthing process went suddenly wrong. I remember, with a shudder the first difficult delivery in an out-lying farm-house.

It was Lucy's second baby which should have been straight forward, but it was a big baby and delivery was slow and latterly obstructed at the pelvic outlet. She had been in labour for many hours.

"Don't push anymore," instructed Jenny the midwife. Lucy was exhausted from her prolonged effort to deliver her new off-spring and her blood pressure was climbing dangerously high.

"We will help it out and all will be okay," as she prepared the outlet-forceps and handed them to me.

This simple request was now well beyond Lucy's control and the next big pain had her pushing strenuously to force the baby through the birth canal. The foetal pulse dropped dramatically and I had to get the baby out promptly. Mother and baby were now in serious trouble. I slipped one arm of the forceps past the head and struggled mightily, then craftily, to advance the other, so that they could be approximated with gentle downward pressure exerted, to encourage the descent of the head. Lucy, despite the midwife's injunctions, was pushing hard into her pelvis, jamming the baby's head against the pelvic wall and leaving no space for the forceps blade.

With brow wet with sweat, I strived to inch the forceps blade into position and doubts of a successful outcome crept into mind. In a moment of panic, I rashly shouted at poor Lucy.

"Stop pushing now! I'll do the pushing, "words which dropped into a sudden void of silence. Lucy and Jenny were taken aback at my sudden loss of composure and Lucy relaxed for a few moments. The left blade of the forceps slipped upward and towards its neighbour and I manipulated them together and started downward traction.

"Steady.Push now," Jenny encouraged Lucy's cooperation.

In a few minutes the baby's head rotated a little for an easier delivery and then, with a whoosh, the delivery was completed.

Jenny took over and I carried the new baby to mum. She was ecstatic and announced proudly,

"We are calling him after you doctor. Thank you for all your help." The interrupted night had brought reward and personal satisfaction. Such appreciation would occur several times over the years and as I drove home in the dawn, I ruminated that while Town Councillors have streets named after them, attending doctors may be recorded in posterity through the naming of a new infant. There was however a personal price to pay for popularity for child births and protracted labours seemed to come in spates and professional demands were exhausting.

"Another successful delivery doctor" Jenny said quietly as she cleaned the instruments, ignoring my emotive outburst of angst.

"We make a good team," I replied. She was an excellent midwife, calm competent and caring. It suddenly occurred to me that when maternity visits were in high demand, I often spent more time with her, often in the wee, small hours of morning, than at home with my wife

Extensive clinical experience would come to me with the passing of the years, with happy outcomes and adverse events, but general medical practice would remain stimulating. As one infection or malady was prevented, or cured, another would arise. Infant and maternal mortality dropped dramatically with improved nutrition and safer working practice. Antibiotics and vaccinations ensured most people lived to retiral. People lived longer, but many did so in poor health and age-degeneration created new demands on the practitioner. Patient encounters were challenging, some humorous, others poignant and sad with all illuminating the rich fabric of human existence. Patients had tales to tell, depositing a rich lode of events in the bedrock of my memory, to mine in time to come.

Town Surgery

The Harborough surgery provided non-appointment consultations through much of the day. Intruding obstetric calls and house visits ensured busy practice. War-time afflictions, poor work practices, inadequate previous health care, social and clinical problems, all brought a plethora of patient presentations to challenge the doctor.

Parking my very basic Renault 4L car carefully in the car park, it stood forlornly beside large, shiny black limousines and a zippy, bright red sportster, belonging to GP. partners, I grasped my shiny new instrument bag and strode towards Grove Surgery, on my first working day in the group health centre, My fellow junior partner and owner of the sports car stepped out to greet me warmly

"Pleased to meet you again, Dr. Welman," then, "sturdy little work-horse," he commented kindly, patting the Renault on the bonnet. His next words however disturbed my bonhomie.

"You have not picked the best time to start in practice. We are all about to resign from the health service." in a dispute with the Government,

British doctors antagonised by Government health policies, had been instructed by the British Medical Association, to sign a post-dated letter indicating withdrawal from the embryonic National Health Service within six months. This threat, if challenged, would have proved a bluff for no doctor of my acquaintance would have ever actually gone on strike, On my surgery desk, the form awaited signature. After long years of preparatory medical school study, I had just crossed the threshold to become a professional health-carer and immediately faced unemployment and penury. Most principals still worked partly in private practice and could afford this gesture of independence.

I had only one private patient on my personal list and would wait without salary for three months, until the quarterly partnership cheque arrived. There was now no certainty others would follow. We were heavily in debt having borrowed funds to cover car purchase, practice-share and house mortgage. Fortunately, after five months of increasing anxiety, a new NHS contract was negotiated, which revolutionised general medical care and resolved the dispute before I became bankrupt.

In addition to "The Grove," there was Hillfoot branch surgery near my home and another at Harside. A visit to the latter involved a sixty mile return trip through winding narrow lanes and manoeuvres through wall-skirted, shrub-topped, upgraded bridal-ways. En route were a multiplicity of little villages, their names prefixed with "upper, lower, mid," and a confusion of hamlets "on, off and beside the burn." In days before satellite navigation systems, their location and route-finding was a nightmare. Rural house calls could involve miles of tricky lane driving, some traversed by heavy trucks carrying stone from adjacent quarries. I often made the journey in the small hours of the morning half-asleep and only came to full wakefulness, when reaching the garage, with no recollection of the intervening journey, or its hazards. House-call requests often came at third–hand, with messages sometimes almost incomprehensible.

"Our Jeannie/Johnnie/Peggy is hanging," was common. I initially believed that there had been a suicide and travelled post haste to the scene to find that, in the local vernacular, a "hanging child" was one that was off food or, had a slight fever. I learned to procrastinate in response to these frequent calls but, was badly misled one day when the telephone message from a relative was,

"Can you come and see our John. He's hanging, "in a voice devoid of urgency. When I finally visited the farm late on the rounds, I was welcomed warmly by the family. When questioned about John his sister responded unemotionally that,

"He's "hanging."

"Where is he? I asked.

"Round in the barn," as they returned to their work! I marvelled at how countrymen would carry on with their work despite illness. In this case however, he was indeed hanging in the barn. He had climbed up on a trestle, tied himself with baling-rope to the rafters and looped it round his neck before stepping to his death. The body was swaying gently in the breeze, while the family prioritised farm duties.

Letters sent by patients to the doctor could also be almost incomprehensible. One of the first which awaited my arrival needed interpretation from Collette the receptionist. Written on a scrap of paper torn from a child's school exercise book it read,with scant punctuation,

"Don't fling mrs O'Hare off the panel after all her sister will soon be on a wheelchair and she is also menalay hany capped and puir Ann is waiting to go to the looniebin. She has also a Drunking husband and Cathleen run off and left her with the 2 Children that poor woman worked hard all her days and thiss is what she gets. do what you like with me Because I am Diying anny way please Doctor Don't put mary off the panel She coulkd not find another doctor."

This epistle took some deciphering and I called on the receptionist for enlightenment. Collette was a pleasant, energetic practice secretary, the "do it all" who, typed, filed, managed partners and had an encyclopaedic knowledge of practice patients. In pre-computer days, given the briefest of details of an individual, she would spirit up their records and provide a detailed rundown on the person and family which amazed me.

A poor memory ensured that I regularly forgot patient names, or recalled distorted addresses. Patients were very forgiving. If the appointment record on my desk was awry, I could easily mix up patient names. The individual concerned would invariably allow me to address them through the consultation as "Mrs. Anderson", or whatever, when the name was Jones, A later telephone call from Colette or Joe Hall, the long-suffering pharmacist, would question whether the name on prescription was correct and I would belatedly realise my error.

Collette rallied to the challenge on this particular occasion.

"It's from Mrs. McGregor. She's an old harridan" she testified. "She's grandmother in a large family and pesters the doctors with demands for unnecessary house calls. Her daughter fell out with Dr. Harley your predecessor and he threatened to put her off the list. "We never did,." she added

"I'll see to it - I replied - We shouldn't put people off, no matter what a nuisance they are."

Although a literary disaster, the letter provided a potted history of a dysfunctional family–one of several I would inherit. Mrs. McGregor was a prolific, if illiterate, writer of notes. She was a doughty lady of vast proportions. Usually flanked by two or three fractious youngsters, she wheezed her way regularly into my surgery consultations, to wheedle cough mixtures and liniments for the tribe of unruly grand-children. The single consultation invariably embraced the many ailments of the brood and wrecked the timing of the appointment system.

If I refused her entreaties, another ungrammatical, obfuscating letter would come my way. They usually referred to her impending death, which was a long time coming. She and the off-spring plagued me for years before she succumbed to infection in an influenza epidemic. We missed her weird epistles and diatribes. Despite her foibles she was a caring grandmother who lived to see her progeny benefit from the schooling she had missed and many graduated from university.

"On-call "evenings at "The Grove" were onerous and I would linger in the main surgery in Harborough to save repeating the ten-mile return journey from home for local calls. One of the patients lived close at hand. Mrs Newton was the local do-gooder. She always looked gaunt and ill, accentuated by a sallow, colourless skin. Convinced she had pernicious anaemia, I checked her health status thoroughly and never found any underlying cause. She was a hypochondriac who needed constant health reassurance. Regular home visit requests were made more acceptable however.

"The kettle is on and you will have a quick cup of tea doctor "she would always greet me.

"I have just baked a cake." She was an excellent baker and beguiled by large helpings of her various culinary gems my visits became weekly.

Alf, her husband, was an ex-regimental sergeant major in the Royal Corp of Music who proudly played the trumpet at Armistice Day parades. Although aged in his eighties, he walked erect with shoulders back and chin-in, as if still on parade.

"I'm getting short of breath." he admitted on one of my visits. On examination I realised he was clinically in heart failure. This diagnostic label one did not then share with patients as they assumed death was imminent. "Your heart is a bit tired" I advised Alf.

"It will see me out" he replied calmly with a jovial grin. My medications lessened his dyspnoea, but his wind instrument playing days were over. Reconciled to his breathing restriction he observed,

"The wife will be pleased if I give up the trumpet."

He had also had played a saxophone in a jazz band for many years and announced he was looking for a successor to care for his beloved instrument.

"Have a go doctor," he offered one day on my home visit. To humour him, I hefted the tenor saxophone and gave a few tentative blows. A few raucous screeches came from the instrument.

"Purse your lips", he ordered.

I had another blow. A few raspberries followed then recognisable notes resulted, as I tightened my lips. "You have the making of a musician." He stated enthusiastically. Less sure of this attribute, I recalled hated hours of piano lessons as a small child. He volunteered nevertheless to teach me saxophone expertise, while I was 'on - call'. A hard taskmaster he proved to be and I had to practise scales and embouchure until lips bled. Soon I came to dread his patient,

"Now we'll jist be havin' that again lad," after a further painful rendition of a set piece.

I practised in the empty consulting room late into the evenings. It was located next to the undertaker's parlour and the screeches and squeals coming from the tortured instrument escaped the room confines. Ultimately, with newly-acquired skills, I was accepted into the local ceilidh band. The undertaker was the drummer.

"I could hear you perform when I was laying them out. It was almost enough to waken the dead," he said wryly.

Anna was another hypochondriac. She lived close to my senior GP partner. Hamish tolerated her high demand for after-surgery hours house calls and would pop in to see her on a social visit. Her visits however meant a 15 mile round trip for me, acceptable in emergency, but her calls were for trivialities. She had been a secretary and had fallen in love with her married boss. After a prolonged clandestine relationship, which she had hoped would ultimately lead to marriage, her paramour had chosen to stay with his wife.

Anna went to pieces, threw up her job and took to her bed. An over-caring and doting mother met her every need and command and so began Anna's bed-bound sojourn. An attractive young woman in her early thirties she could have found another partner, but chose to dwell on her lost love affair. Her disturbed emotions consolidated into psychological disturbance. Long before I arrived in the village, her role as an ill woman with physical disability was well established. Her medical record covered many pages. Complaints had long frustrated family doctors who had referred her to countless medical consultants, who, found nothing physically wrong with her. Her affliction was all in the mind. Freed from work stressors, with no demands upon her and waited on by an abetting Mum, she had found a role as a chronically-ill sufferer,.

Mother was a small mouse of a woman totally dominated by Anna and convinced of her daughter's illness chronicity. Her pinched, worried face was accentuated by the tight bun clenching back her hair. She fetched and carried by night and day, while Anna prettied herself, read books and paid court to village visitors taken in by her list of complaints.

"It's our Anna. In terrible pain doctor, she needs you right away, "would come the telephone call, and I would try to wriggle out of another visit. She would insist on the urgency of her request, and once again I would angrily attend the daughter. Irrespective of the hour, Anna, recumbent in bed, with face and hair impeccably groomed, always greeted me belligerently.

"You took your time. My back is killing me."

"Poor dear, the pain is dreadful." Mother would add in support.

I sometimes wished unprofessionally that the pain would have a fatal outcome, but Anna was set to annoy me for a long time. Physically intact, but bed-bound for many days, she was beginning to suffer from infirmities due to immobility. Muscles were thinning, joints weakening and she was getting bed- sores. A return to normal mobility would have reversed this deteriorating process, but she had convinced herself and those around her of her incapacity.

"I cannot stand the pain. Any movement is torture." She would reiterate, but her features belied any physical agony.

Anna had a not unpleasant personality until it came to discussion of her physical and mental condition when she was inured to logical discussion. She was well read - too well acquainted with medical knowledge - for she idled away her hours in bed-repose by reading up medical books. She was often better aware of the symptomatology of her supposed medical conditions than the attending doctor.

Over time, she had acquired and presented the symptoms of many illnesses. She queened over the village despite her exclusion from social events, knew all the gossip and was regularly visited by villagers intent on catching up with the intrigues of village politics. Convinced she was a very ill woman, any attempt to undermine her position as a chronic invalid was resisted. Whenever she was feeling down, which usually occurred in the early evening when her neighbours were settling into a round of social events, Anna would be struck by some phantom symptom. Brought to the attention of Mum, she would invariably call for medical aid. Anna quickly became a "Heart-sink" patient for me. The first words of her mother's telephone call had my heart sink profoundly in my chest. A battle of words and wills was about to ensue.

On my first visit, met at the door by fawning mother and shown to the best-room where tea and scones awaited on a tray, I foolishly believed that I might succeed where many others had failed. Dressed in a frothy pink, flower-bud-embellished dressing gown Anna was at her most charming when I reached the bedside. Facial make-up was immaculate and no hair was out of place. She had the time and the hours to preen and perfect her personal appearance. Her well-rehearsed symptoms seemed genuine. She avidly accepted treatment if offered, until discussion of mobilisation, even to a chair by the bedside, which was vigorously resisted and brought immediate refusal.

"I cannot stand Doctor, and any movement is intensely painful. The hospital doctors have tried everything but I just get worse. Oh, the pain, when I so much as turn. It's dreadful. Isn't that right Mother?"

"Mum confirmed her words. "Terrible screams when we try to move her from bed. She is in agony Doctor."

My full neurological examination of her limbs and thorough check of her body systems revealed no abnormality other than thinning and weakening of muscles generated by months in bed. I recognised that the indomitable Anna would not be cured by my administrations. Her problems were psychological and psychiatrists had washed their hands off her after failed attempts to alter her behaviour. Anna had found a safe, secure, non-threatening niche in which to live. No one was going to dislodge her from her self-determined role. My frequent visits in my partner's absence grew more frustrating and our relationship more strained.

"It's our Anna, she is in great pain and she needs a visit Doctor, "would come the wheedling voice of Mum over the telephone and latterly I was tempted to have her pass on a divine message..

"Get up out of your bed and walk!"

Usually, I grudgingly made the long journey, scolded her for wasting my time, tried to educate Mum into separating legitimate medical need from imagined malady and put her down for a visit next day from her own long-suffering doctor. I became reconciled to having Anna as a noose round my neck until one of us left this earth. I suspected I might be first to go. Strangely, she never sought powerful analgesics or addictive drugs. She was satisfied with simple remedies as long as her bed enthronement was not threatened. I concluded that the only way to force change on the household was to separate mother and daughter. Mum howeverwould not contemplate a respite-break and Anna would have a hysterical fit if the possibility was discussed.

Months went by and my rancour became anger and finally acceptance that, some burdens in life one cannot change. Then, I thought salvation had finally come. Mum fell down the stairs and broke her hip bone. In my partner's absence on holiday, I perfidiously discouraged Anna's transfer to a care home.

"Now she will have to get up," I gloated. To my surprise, the villagers rallied round and set up a care rota to maintain her dependent existence. They responded to the invalid's perceived needs. A procession of villagers cared for her, until Mum once again took her fetch and care place by her daughter's side. Anna maintained her out-of-hours home-call requests, which continued to infuriate me, as it was a "shrink", or saint she needed, not a GP.

"I do not need a psychiatrist, "she would object. "I need a GP who will care for me. I need my own doctor, "she would aver pointedly. Hamish my partner, unwilling to antagonise the patient and his village neighbours, continued to over-medicalise her complaints and she remained a thorn in my side.

The years of immobility finally began to take their toll however. Anna began to have legitimate symptomatology resulting from her prolonged bed-bound state. House call requests began to be genuine needs and could now be met with conventional if inadequate treatment. Thinning of the bones, kidney stones, skin ulcers and preventive care and treatment brought iatrogenic illness and Anna began to fade away. Always a slender lady she became wraithlike despite the devoted administrations of Mum.

Villagers were a constant support and the stream of visitors steady. She was finally hospitalised, operated upon, developed drug-resistant pneumonia and died. Villagers perceived her as a martyr to ill health and turned out en masse to her funeral - a self-inflicted demise. Anna's premature death brought her mother's release from continual care. Sadly, freed from a role of devotion, she herself just disintegrated and shortly died, to follow her offspring. Fellow partners felt a guilty relief at Anna's final passing. My car visit mileage fell dramatically and her death was one I did not lament.

Stimulated perhaps by Anna's neurotic pathology and attracted to the psychology and psychiatry disciplines, I took up an attachment at the local Psychiatric Hospital - a former lunatic asylum- (the "loonie bin" to the locals). It held most of the county's mentally ill, still then labelled as "of insane mind". The discipline was embryonic with enlightenment to come in future years. Pathologically disturbed, dementing, social misfits and intellectually retarded people were held together in one unit. They drifted round large wards like flotsam on the tide. Patients were restrained in locked wards and restraining chairs and many were blasted with near-lethal doses of electricity in electro-convulsive therapy.

Some of the doctors were weird in dress and mannerisms and their behaviour not always easy to differentiate from that of patients. Nurses were uniformed and prowled the wards clutching great rings of keys, the symbol of their authority.

There were few female psychiatrists but one, an Indian lady, was practising hypnotherapy which had only recently been accepted by the British Medical Association as a legitimate means of treatment. Impressed by the efficacy of her treatment, I enrolled on a course to master the art, which I would practise on selected cases over my clinical career.

This proved a useful skill. as only half of practice patients had a physical disorder. Many a physical presentation masked psychological disturbance. Medical school had poorly prepared for the anxiety states, depression and behavioural disorders which manifested so predominantly in primary health care. I was often surprised how "the power of the mind" could be harnessed in therapy and bring cure for many entrenched psychological conditions.

Power of the Mind

"There is a call from the Townends", Ann said slightly defensively as I returned home from a consulting session. "There seems to be a problem with the children, but the message was passed by a neighbour who gave no details." She knew that I liked as much information as possible before doing 'out-of-hour' calls, to ensure I had appropriate medications with me. We usually dispensed drugs from the bag when the local pharmacy was closed.

The Townsend family lived in Haughside, a poor urban area of the practice, where many socially-deprived families had their homes. The majority were decent folk. Many, unemployed miners, had lost employment with the closure of a local pit. Few now had a job and unselective TV-watching dominated their day. Neighbourhood families all had acquired colour television sets before Ann and I owned one. Greyhound and pigeon-racing were dominant interests and many had a pigeon-loft in the back garden. Most were entitled to a ton of free coal, delivered each month.

An evening approach to their homes was always hazardous. Great piles of coal had been abandoned on the poorly-lit road by delivery wagons. Recipients were disinclined to barrow it into coal-sheds and the heaps often caused an obstruction for weeks. Coal-dust blew around the street. One such unlit heap blocked entry to the Townsend house on my approach, threatening to trip me. The street lamps had all been vandalised.

On previous visits, I found that some coal had finally reached Jessie's house to be stored in the bath. This was a house where a call to see a child in the evening could prove an unenlightening experience. There was usually only one viable light in the house and it was never in the bedroom of the patient. It usually illuminated the living-room, where the family clustered round the TV. Often the patient had to be examined by torch-light, as the alternative was to remove the sole light source and plunge the house into darkness during the examination.

Many extended families occupied these houses with bedraggled, worked-to-death mothers caring for kids and husbands, who succumbed to chronic bronchitis and early death. Mere maternal drudges, largely constrained to household chores, some were abused by drunken spouses who spent the weekly social benefit on drink. Jessie Townsend was one such long-suffering woman, driven almost beyond endurance by unending family demands. She had grown up in the home of a local banker and had the misfortune to fall in love with a handsome young-lay about. His good looks belied a natural tendency to sloth and devious ways. Jessie had married against her parents' wishes and they had cut off all contact with her. In the early years of the marriage her work brought in an income to support them both. With the arrival of an ever-increasing family and a debauched, work-shy husband, they had become dependent upon state welfare benefits.

Family members were regular surgery visitors and its size increased annually at a time when the efficient oral contraception still lay in the future. The children were poorly dressed in others' discards. They invariably had runny noses and sometimes purple-dyed heads where the district nurse had treated them for impetigo skin infection. Jessie was a poor-looking unkempt soul, dressed in Charity Shop cast-offs and with wind-tossed hair that rarely saw the brush. The family, although not particularly unruly, made demands upon her she could not meet.

I struggled into the darkened hallway, guided only by flickering light from the television set in the living room. I wondered which of the six children would be unwillingly prised away from the TV, so that I could use my pen-torch to illuminate swollen tonsils. The condition which to permanently afflict her children.

"OK .Who is the culprit tonight?" I asked the throng whose attention was glued to the screen, as Jessie was not in sight.

To my surprise, I was greeted by husband Jock, who rarely frequented the home. When I had asked his whereabouts previously, one of the children would invariably respond,

"He's at the dugs."He would be spending some of the sparse family funds on dog-racing.

"Jessie's gone," he stated woefully, "and left me wi' a' the weans. I cannae manage them. You'll hae t' dae somethin' aboot it. She just goat up an' went." he lamented.

"Aye, Ma's gone," came as a chorus from the horde distracted momentarily from the TV soap opera.

"You'll need to git help, or I'll dae masel,' in", dad added soulfully. This unfolding personal drama did not retain family interest and TV activity again absorbed the offspring's attention.

Jessie had apparently walked off without explanation, leaving Jock and children.

"This is a case for the social worker. I advised thankfully; keen to continue my visits and feeling that the realities of child-care might have him finally appreciate his wife's burden.

The social-work department's response was leisurely, delayed and dilatory and his dilemma attracted scant attention until three days later, he himself absconded.

"Mum's oot and dad's awa, "the family assured the visiting social worker." He'll no be back, but she'll no' be lang," they chorused to questions from Mrs. Bellwether, the poorly-trained and incompetent social worker who made a cursory visit to the household. She failed to recognise or report the family's needs to her department head and they fell beneath the bureaucratic radar.

Unfazed, older children, who were in their late teens, found part-time jobs and cared for the younger ones.

"We can mind fir oorsels." Sarah the oldest teenager assured me on a rare visit to the surgery, and mind for themselves they did. They attended school, scrounged a living and survived. The youngest was taken in by neighbours to be looked after on a volitional basis by local families, until old enough to be cared for by siblings. In a remarkable display of self-sufficiency and neighbourly goodwill, the family managed their lives and prospered by graft and wit.

Many years later, when acting as locum for a GP friend in a neighbouring town, a very, well-dressed and mannered lady turned up in surgery with her smart partner. I felt I should know her, but had difficulty with the recollection.

"I know you," I ventured tentatively. Rather sheepishly she admitted to her identity.

"I used to be Jessie Townsend." She had escaped from the relentless family toil and made a remarkably good second life for herself.

"I was at my wit's end doctor and Jock was not pulling his weight. I left the house to shop and don't remember anything. I ended up in Newcastle. Did not know who I was or where I came from, for months. When I did remember, I did not let on. I have a new life now, "she said defensively. "The kids have done well and Jock drank himself to death." She had apparently been in a fugue – a defensive mental state that had divorced her from reality. Surprisingly, despite the deprived environment and lack of parental affection, the children had done well. Independent-minded, they escaped the poverty and depravation of their early upbringing, acquired good jobs and were successfully reared families in an environment previously denied to them.

Hysterical Paralysis

Her visit reminded me of another hard-working soul devoted to a very large family, living in a street close to the Townsend home. Emily Jones' devoted home making endeavours were little appreciated by her many sons and daughters and she toiled away for years at their beck and call. One day she slipped, fell and broke both arms.

"Hospital for you," I said decisively as I surveyed the bone damage after responding to an emergency call.

"At least you will get a rest there," I added. Overnight she was suddenly the centre of attention and the family rallied around to help and do chores. The fractures slowly healed and within days of her recuperation, the familiar dependency on Mum took over again. Some months later there was another house call.

"I have lost the use in my arm." She reported. "I have no power in it at all."

I could find no medical cause for this, but fearing stroke or brain disease responded cautiously and advised,

"A hospital check-up for you and some tests."

Once again the siblings came to her aid, but within a few days, when power had returned, she found herself again at every one's beck and call. Again, a short time later, she was further assailed by loss of power in lower limbs. The pattern of disability became repetitive and I believed this to be a functional complaint and a psychological disorder. The diagnosis did not satisfy the family.

Distraught, her relatives called upon physicians and neurologists for an alternative diagnosis. In the absence, of any physiological pathology she was told that she had a hysterical condition which was causing loss of function. I tried to explain the position to her,

"You are not coping with all the pressures upon you and your mind is acting defensively to protect you. You are not paralysed but you think that you are."

She could not accept this explanation

"I just cannot move my legs," she insisted," then suddenly the power comes back and it goes again. "

Once again the centre of the attention, with sibling support, she had much to gain from her condition. A pattern of behaviour began to emerge. She would recover normal function temporarily, until family demands became too onerous and then hysterical malfunction took over. Gradually, spells of normality got less and less and she ultimately became wheel-chair-bound as muscles and nerves wasted. In time, she became totally reliant upon external care and in a role reversal, was dependent upon a family who grudgingly gave her the support she had long given them.

She was finally admitted to the community hospital, to the geriatric ward, although only aged fifty. There was no other suitable rehabilitation unit. I had worked there for some years in addition to full time general practice, adding to an already heavy work-load. Hospital practice however helped to keep me aware of medical management advances. Kate Stammers, a new consultant geriatrician, had recently arrived on the scene, determined to clear her wards of "bed blockers", which this lady now undoubtedly had become. This rather derogatory term described patients who were occupying acute admission beds, when they should have been placed in a convalescent or rehabilitation unit, which were always full.

In general conversation one day, when discussing the case on the consultant ward-round, Jennie wondered,

"Perhaps there is a role here for hypnosis. The psychiatrists sometime use it in patients with hysterical symptoms." Nursing-sister Kay Ring – widely referred to by patient as "the caring sister" after she married the ward physiotherapist Jeremy Ring - encouraged this line of thought.

"Dr. Welman does hypnosis," she volunteered. I quailed as I had not publicised this personal clinical interest. The British Medical Association had only recently recognised hypnosis as a potentially useful means of treating patients. Many doctors remained sceptical as to its restorative properties. They still associated it with the denounced art of "animal magnetism" once practiced by Mesmer. a German psychologist. Medical practitioners who dabbled in its use were often viewed with dubiety

"I have tried it. Iin a few cases," haltingly, as I tried to deflect the suggestion, but Kate was not going to pass up the opportunity to gain a bed-release.

"How did it go? Was it successful?"

"It works very well, "Kay jumped in before I could muster a rejoinder. "He cured me." and to my embarrassment, she recited the tale of her treatment for a phobia of tunnels. She had been one of the first of my patients to benefit from newly acquired hypnotherapeutic skills

Kate responded enthusiastically. "Why do you not give it a go? It would be wonderful if it worked." She saw an opportunity to treat a patient seen by many doctors and submitted to over-much investigation. All confirmed that her condition was imagined and had no physical or pathological basis.

I had always been very selective in choice of patients for hypnotherapy and had chosen conditions responsive to treatment, in patients highly motivated to positively respond. This lady was one to be avoided. She had an entrenched, adaptive condition which protected her from the over-demands of the family situation, there was little incentive to change her behaviour. I tried to avoid a commitment. With a new consultant and the focus of ward nurses and doctors, it was difficult to deny that she might indeed respond to trance-induction therapy. Hoist with my own petard, I hoped that Emily would resist further treatment.

"I believe we can make you better Mrs. Jones and get you back to normal again," Kate advised her. "Dr.Welman has suggested a new treatment".

To my chagrin, she willingly agreed to further therapy..

"I will try anything Doctor. I just want to get better, "she assured Jennie.

She was bed–fast, being fed and toileted by nurses and had to be taken on a trolley to a treatment room. I had known her in the wards from previous visits and we had a good rapport, but I was the apprehensive one in the ensuing interview. Sigmund Freud the psychologist had done sterling work with hysterical states when he had first gained acceptance for the therapy, not many psychiatrists now used it for hysteria. I had seen no references to its use in entrenched cases such as hers.

Emily was wheeled into a side-ward and lifted on to the bed by two nurses. I approached diffidently.

"If you are feeling comfortable I shall put some suggestions to you and this will help you slip into a very relaxed state beneficial to your well-being. You will not be asleep but in an in between state between full alertness and trance," I put to her, on starting the session.

She went very easily into hypnotic trance and I gave her some suggestions.

"You will feel back in complete control of your life and fending for yourself once again." I added suggestions that if she recovered full use of her limbs again she would also be able to resist over-involvement with the family. She would build a life for herself. I taught her some procedures for taking herself into therapeutic trance, concerned that she might turn her professional dependence on to me.

I then took the plunge and suggested that her immobile right hand, was losing its paralysis and she would soon be able to move it at my signal. The other hand arms and legs were dealt with similarly and when she was completely relaxed, I suggested that she could move them when my fingers were clicked. She responded immediately, with a mass muscular reflex that seemed to lift her off the bed. Legs and arms continued to twitch in uncontrolled fashion. My first reaction was that she had suffered an epileptic seizure, but she had over-ridden the hysterical paralysis and was smiling and saying over and over,
"I can move doctor, I can move!"

She returned to the ward sitting in a wheel-chair and fed herself at the next meal, the first time for many months. Her musculature was weak and physiotherapy was needed to get her fully functional again. She returned home and remained fit and free from medical intervention. The family had perhaps learned from the experience and did not reinstate their former dependence upon her. I remembered agaim the biblical story, where the paralysed patient was instructed to, "take up thy bed and walk."

This case was no miracle. The patient had boxed herself into a corner and either consciously or subconsciously recognised that she was at the end of the road. Her infliction had deposited her in a geriatric ward with the prospect of ending her days surrounded by dementing old people, a daunting prospect. My therapy gave her a way-out without loss of face. She accepted it and never looked back. I was reminded of the words of a grateful patient after I had removed a disabling phobia,

"Quiet words, gentle words, can be effective words and remarkably successful words,"

I had taken up hypnotherapy by chance, after a training attachment to the local psychiatric hospital. Dr Chaudri the resident doctor was an attractive, sari-wearing Asian lady. Women and Asian doctors were both rare within the NHS in those days and her ward-rounds always brought a tail of admiring male students. Some were attracted by her physical allure, but she also practised hypnosis on some of her patients. This was still an innovative procedure with the technique only recognised in treatment by the General Medical Council in 1953. Devina Chaudri encouraged me to try it out after training sessions.

"It is an effective form of psychotherapy." she had assured me." It relies on words and suggestion and patient rapport. You will be surprised by the response.

"Try it." By chance, a possible candidate presented in surgery a few days later and I tentatively selected her as a test case. She had no physical problem, but a psychological one difficult to treat.

"It's my nose doctor. It's getting bigger all the time. I can't go out now for everyone is staring at me."

Miss Love - she had reverted to her maiden name after a messy divorce - had a history of anxiety states. Since separation from her husband, these incidents were becoming more frequent and profound. Repeated absence from work she did not like, now threatened her employment. There were few psychological resources then available within the health care system. I considered additional tranquillisers prescribed by a colleague and rejected the thought. They did nothing to treat the cause of the affliction and often half-drugged the patient without bringing cure.

Amelia Love had become a regular attender. I thought her name incongruous, for I suspected that it was a lack of love and affection that had created her symptoms. An Ear, Nose and Throat Consultant had found no anomaly with her nose and it looked normal to the observer. She would usually present with a minor complaint which took a short time to deal with, then come out with the real motivation for her visit.

"While I am here Doctor," she would announce, just when I was ready to ring for the next patient. This was a common ploy with patients and I thought of it as the "While I am here syndrome". It usually meant an over-run appointment as I dealt with the genuine presenting problem. Repressed symptoms or anxieties would be revealed which were often crucial to diagnosis and many " While I am here, " presentations would often point up serious disease, disorder and cancer, with the reluctant mention of symptoms and signs the patient had feared or ignored.

On this occasion her approach was overt.

"I am going to have to give up work." She stated. "I can't leave home." My heart sank for this would certainly mean house calls in future.

"Pills don't work and they make me sleepy," she continued." Is there nothing else for me to try?"

This was my opportunity.

"There is some treatment which can help this condition," I suggested tentatively,

"Anything." She responded eagerly. "I want to get back to work and lead a normal life."

"Hypnotherapy." I said.

"You mean hypnosis?"

"Yes"

"But is that not for people on the stage?"

"This is medical hypnosis and it only works if you are a willing participant , a good responder, and you will never be required to do anything with which you are not comfortable. "

"Do you put me to sleep?"

"You go into a trance state which is not sleep and not full wakefulness, but in between. It is very health-giving and can bring cure for certain conditions such as yours. You are an attractive woman and if we can reassure you about the shape of your nose, life can be good for you. "

Miss Love responded positively.

"Okay. When can we start? "

"First of all I would like you to listen to this." I had made a tape-recording of the preliminary treatment presentation for patients. She listened carefully and said she was willing to have hypnotherapy.

This was a crucial first case. Success would encourage me to use hypnosis again, but I was dubious of its value and my therapeutic skills with the technique. The procedure despite formal professional recognition was still disdained by many doctors, although it was being used successfully in obstetrics practice.

"Lie down on the couch and close your eyes and think of a place where you have been at peace with yourself in some tranquil scene." I ordered.

She proved to be a good subject and the treatment went smoothly. The obsessive fixation regarding her nose size diminished. Within days she returned to work and I did not see her for many years. She presented again after being made redundant and was struggling to find a job. Her obsessive behaviour was merely dormant and not extinguished as I had hoped.

"It's my chin," she announced. It's a funny shape and it's getting bigger by the day." It looked perfectly normal to me. Again she submitted to hypnosis. Treatment was effective once again.. She found another job and left the area. I hoped her cure was permanent.

Heartened by this success, I continued to use the treatment tool on selected patients over many years in practice, with no adverse sequelae. Patients could be taught to hypnotise themselves. They could recourse to self-therapy when excess psychological demands were made upon them, without the need for medical support. Patient feed-back could be long delayed and there was sometimes a long wait to find the outcome of treatment.

I was attending a concert many years later in the local village hall when I recognised one of the musicians. At the interval I went to speak to him and climbed up on the platform to chat. The next day he rang to advise me that a fellow colleague Jane Player had recognised me and wished to make contact if I provided a telephone number. The name meant nothing to me. Somewhat reluctantly I agreed, wondering if a complaint was coming my way. In due course the lady rang.

"You may not remember me," she started," I only saw you once many years ago, but I have never forgotten your treatment". Apprehensively, I waited her next comment anticipating criticism for some past treatment failure.

"It was wonderful," she said, "and it quite revolutionised my life!"

She identified herself further saying she lived in a nearby village, but I could not remember anything about her.

"Thirty years ago your partner sent me to you for hypnosis treatment. "You gave me one session of therapy and it brought immediate cure. "

I was struggling to remember this episode and teased a few more details from her before recall kindled a dim memory of when she had appeared in the surgery distraught and in despair. Jane was a skilled cellist who played in a national orchestra and had been offered promotion to a leading role. This entailed moving from home and family and she lacked confidence in her ability to meet potential demands on her expertise. A panic state had resulted. She developed a tremor when bowing her instrument. This affected her play and threatened livelihood and promotion.

I had treated her conventionally with ego-strengthening and anxiety-relieving support in a short session and promptly forgot about her under the pressure of busy general medical practice. She had moved south, became section leader of the orchestra and enjoyed an illustrious career before moving back north again. Now she belatedly, but gratefully wanted to acknowledge my fortuitous contribution to her professional success.

The meeting reminded me of the leader of an other renowned orchestra who had presented with a similar problem. He too had benefited from a short therapeutic session and overcome a tremor which could have ruined his professional career. The efficacy of this simple procedure continued to amaze me over the years and I wondered why more doctors did not learn the techniques. One patient always came to mind as an anecdote when I was later teaching classes as a General Practice trainer. It was the end of a long day and even longer surgery consultation list. By 8pm, I was longing for dinner and relaxation by the fireside.

"It's another extra," announced the receptionist and my heart sank.

"She is not one of ours. Do you want to see her?" and I cheered up. I did not contractually have to see this patient.

"She is emigrating tomorrow and needs a note to say she is unfit to travel."

Intrigued and aware that a note would only take a moment to write, I hesitated.

"She really is in a bad state doctor. You will have to see her." I was trapped, so unwillingly, she was added to the waiting list.

In due course, a good-looking, thirty year old, woman came into see me. She was smartly-dressed but her face was streaked with tears, make-up was running and she was very agitated. She introduced herself; Joan Traveller told me her story hesitantly with much prompting. She was a very successful local businesswoman, had prospered financially, met a South African and was going to Capetown to marry him and set up business there. She had sold her shops in Britain, disposed of her home and assets and had tickets for a flight out of the UK the next day. Joan had become ever more emotionally and mentally disturbed in the previous few days.

"The thought of boarding a plane and leaving the ground terrifies me and I can't sleep for thinking about it, "she said, in tears. She had apparently always had a slight phobia of flying, but now it had become critical.

"I would like an insurance note stating I am unfit for travel." This was an easy option for me. She would have been gone from the office in minutes if I complied. I could be en route for dinner and fireside in minutes and was sorely tempted. To qualm my conscience I offered,

"Perhaps a tranquilliser would help?"

"No I do not want to be sedated", as she spurned the offer.

I knew their use would merely treat the symptoms of her malady and not the cause and was not curative. Gradually she calmed down as we talked. Joan was facing a rare crisis in her life which she could not manage. She was normally a very self-possessed woman with good control of her life and perhaps I could help her.

"Hypnotherapy could help you get to South Africa," I said to her. She was surprised, but admitted that a friend had an experience of medical therapy which had been beneficial.

"Will it cure me?" Joan wanted to know. I temporised,

"It often works and I have had many patients overcome a fear of flying when they have had hypnotherapy.

"Okay. I'll have it, she said decisively,

I went through the usual informative procedures and then trance-induction, with suggestions that she would be able to travel calmly the next day. She could overcome the fears she had of her new partnership and change in location. In half an hour she was gone and I could thankfully get home to Ann and family.

Six weeks later she telephoned to say she had experienced an uneventful flight. A year later a Christmas card advised that her marriage and business were thriving and I forgot about the incident. Six years later, at the end of another long day, I saw another name had been added to the list, one which I did not recognise and I rang Collette in reception.

"It's a temp. She says you knew her as Joan Traveller. "Temporary patients were always a nuisance for there were no accompanying notes and it took extra time to deal with them. The name eluded my memory.

"She says you treated her some time ago."

Grudgingly I acceded to the request. The door opened to reveal the South African immigrant. Joan looked very glamorous and was dressed in an elegant costume with matching expensive, hand-bag.

"I was hoping to see you doctor. I have brought you some wine, "said Joan as she dumped a box on the floor beside me.

"I have been doing well and business is good but I need another miracle cure.

"Why what has happened?" and her features darkened.

"I was subjected to an attempted rape in a shopping centre in Johannesburg. I got away and am physically okay, but my fear of flying has returned. I have had to come back by sea to see you!"

We chatted about her life abroad, then, I once again repeated the procedure of six years previously and off she went. Once again some weeks later, there was a call to say,

"All was well. I am flying again. Thanks to you." She never returned.

Hypnosis was known to be an effective way of treating the very common fear of flying and an unusual opportunity had presented for me to try the method out. I was flying down on the scheduled flight to London en route to a Medical Conference. By chance, I was seated beside John Speed, the regional manager of a drug company. As we took off John exhibited all the signs of panic associated with a flying phobia and I offered some calming comments. He hesitantly revealed he was about to lose his job, as his fear of flight was interfering with the ability to do his work which involved much air travel. He had been spending many hours driving round the UK to avoid flying. His company had warned him that he must use aeroplanes, or they would dismiss him. Without contemplating what I was doing, I continued to talk to him encouraging him to drift into a hypnotic trance, with suggestions of how he would overcome his fears and deal with his anxieties and maintain his employment. He called into the surgery some later to happily advise,

"I made the return air trip successfully and continue to fly around the country. Thanks Doc". In extremis with a little psychological help, he had dug into his own mental resources to counter his fear. Once again, "Quiet words proved effective words and remarkably successful." He was a bee-keeper and regularly thereafter a pot of fresh honey would arrive for me with a succinct note, "Still flying."

Telepathy

One successful hypnotic procedure, although successful, did leave me feeling slightly guilty. The call came at 3am.I had attended to a prolonged obstetric delivery earlier and after a succession of interrupted nights on duty was feeling tired and weary. The strident ringing of the bedside telephone jolted me reluctantly from sleep.

"Doctor." I croaked.

"It's James Sullivan doctor. I am sorry to bother you but Lilly is really bad." I knew James well .He was a pleasant, young, hard-working cable-jointer with a telephone company diligently working his way through life and providing for his new wife. They had been childhood playmates and he had always lovingly cared for her as she was a bronchial asthmatic. She severe attacks of breathlessness. Asthma was poorly understood in these days and there was little in the way of therapy. One or two drugs like adrenaline could be given in serious attacks, but the medicines could themselves be toxic and people died from bronchial spasm.

Unusually, thanks to his job, the Sullivans' had not only a house-telephone, but an extension into the bed-room and as I came reluctantly to my senses, I could hear Lilly's strident, rasping wheeze and breathing.

"She is a bad colour Doctor" said a worried James. I reacted slowly, looking for an excuse to avoid a visit. The thought of exchanging the warmth of bed for exposure to an ice-cold winter night was unappealing.

"Has she taken all her pills? I asked,

"Yes...and her inhaler?

"Yes and I have steamed her."

He knew the treatment procedures and a visit was clearly necessary. I steeled myself to make an emergency call. Then a thought came to mind. I remembered that Lilly had heard about the use of hypnotherapy in childbirth. She had encouraged me to teach her the procedure for delivery of her baby many months previously. She felt that it had also helped her breathing and had said she would continue to practise self-hypnosis. I had not seen her recently. In a despairing attempt to avoid a visit I said,

"James , let me speak to Lilly."

"Doctor . I am so sorry to trouble you," she wheezed struggling for breath. The Sullivans always appreciated the NHS and did not like to bother me although their needs were always genuine.

"Do you remember how you went into trance in the surgery? " I asked Lilly.

"Yes. But I have not been practising because I was so much better. "she replied.

"Well, Can we go through the induction again. " I suggested.

"Yes please," she responded.

"Well. Just start visualising that special place where you feel at peace with yourself ....," I instructed.

Then I quietly continued the process advising that her breathing was easing and she would fall asleep and waken up feeling well in the morning. I then put the phone down and promptly fell asleep myself. Three hours later, a further house-call request awakened me. A teenager had acute abdominal pain and when I visited, had signs of acute appendicitis. I sent him to hospital. This emergency over, I thought guiltily about Lilly and her asthma attack. Avoiding her visit was unethical and I worried that she might have deteriorated. I turned the car and drove to her house. All was dark and I had a nagging concern that James had rushed her to the emergency unit. I rang the doorbell and waited apprehensively. There was a delayed response until a sleepy and surprised husband appeared.

"How Is Lilly?" I blurted out, fearing the worse.

"In bed." he said," after you spoke to her the wheeze went away and she dozed off."

"I was passing and thought I would look in," I added defensively. Relieved at his words, I advanced to the bed-room where his wife was sleeping peacefully and breathing normally.

Simple psychotherapy had worked telephonically and my guilt dissipated. I could and perhaps should have been criticised for not attending Lilly at home, but she was delighted with the treatment and James welcomed the tardy visit, made only to assuage a guilty conscience.

Although many illnesses require modern medication and surgical intervention, a large number of the patients in my general medical practice needed psychotherapeutic support, which was rarely available in those days. Simple psychological procedures and authoritarian "suggestions" could be powerful tools in helping many patents overcome their mental upsets. They often proved more durable treatments than conventional medical intervention.

Canine Encounters

Tommy Shirker was a council employee who worked intermittently on refuse collection. A heavy thickset and muscular man, he was work-shy and his work record was punctuated by absences. A heavy drinker and devotee of the local public house, his heavy beer-swilling sessions were invariably followed by a day off work. A chronic bronchitis sufferer, with a condition aggravated by a chain smoking habit, he used the disorder to claim sickness benefit. As he rarely surfaced after a nocturnal alcoholic binge in time for morning surgery, he regularly demanded a house call. In days when these were rarely refused, the request was reluctantly accepted by the receptionist and a more reluctant call made by myself. His long-suffering wife had finally divorced him after he beat her up once too often in a drunken rage. He now lived alone in a council estate house. The door-entry was up several steps with a right-hand turn to the house door guarded by a low wall.

I arrived at his home in a disgruntled mood after a night interrupted by menial calls, followed by long, tedious morning surgery consultations. The call-list was long and I anticipated another fruitless visit to Tommy. Our relationship had always been fraught, as I felt his house calls unjustified. He considered them his right and an obligation on the NHS. rather than a privilege. My attempts to change his behaviour had consistently fallen on deaf ears.

As I climbed the stairs and approached the door which was ajar, I prepared to do verbal battle once again. It was my habit when visiting to ring the bell if there was one, bang on the door, shout out "Doctor" and enter the house without ceremony, as I was obviously expected. This occasionally led to unforeseen events. A disembodied voice would advise, "the rent is on the mantle," or, "the meter is in the cupboard." I then had to work my way through the house room by room to find the patient.

On one unfortunate occasion, I did not write down the address for the house call as I believed I knew the location. Arriving in a residential area of many streets lined with similar bungalows, I turned the car into a drive, approached the house and followed my usual casual visit routine calling out, "Doctor," as I entered. There was no answer to my call and assuming the patient was asleep, I climbed the stairs to the bed-rooms and opened the door to one. There was a recumbent figure on the bed and presuming this to be the patient, I approached, called quietly again, "Doctor "and patted a sheet-enshrouded body.

There was a delayed response and sitting down on the bed, I rubbed an exposed shoulder vigorously. A tousle-haired, sleepy-eyed woman rolled over and peered up at me. There was an unbelieving silence for a few moments as I realised that the lady was not my patient and as she came to terms with having an intruder in her bed-room sitting on the bed. I recoiled, coming hastily to my feet, suddenly aware I was in the wrong house. Thoughts of litigation and criminal arrest flooded my mind. Many women would have screamed at the intrusion but, with great equanimity she merely said,

"Oh, It's you Doctor, it will be my neighbour you are looking for. She is one house further up the street." Embarrassed, I stuttered an apology and attempted amends before hastily escaping to make the appropriate house visit.

I had been fortunate, as Bet Whyte was a staff-nurse who worked night shifts in the local infirmary. Despite being wakened in the middle of her slumbers, she had identified me and had the sangfroid to recognise my error and calmly redirect me. Few young women I suspected would have acted so placidly and helped me retain professional decorum. For a time thereafter, I would await an invitation after a peremptory door knock or bell-ring. Time-pressures from long house call lists soon had me revert to habitual behaviour and barge in to houses after a single, brief door knock.

This almost led to serious personal physical mishap on this visit to Tommy. In this case, I knew the address was correct and bounded up the steps to the door-entry and thrust open the door to breeze in. A voice from deep within the house was accompanied by the ominous rattling of a heavy chain, which pulled me up promptly.

"The dug will nae hairm ye," Tommy bellowed and with these words a snarling Alsatian dog hurtled along the passage and launched itself at me. I reversed direction with alacrity. Fast as I was, the dog was faster. I was pinned against the external retaining wall opposite the door. The beast was on me, with slavering mouth and jaw-full of teeth going for my throat. I hastily leaned backward and the animal's fangs flashed before me at eye-level. The bite missed my facial anatomy by an inch. Teeth however caught the front of my new coat and the falling dog, jaw clenched on fabric, ripped all the buttons from the garment.

Jammed against the wall, I was at the beast's mercy for its next attack, but there came further clanking of chain, and a plethora of curses. Chain, with dog, was pulled firmly back in to the house. I followed apprehensively to reach the kitchen where Tony was sitting wheezing in a chair, one leg of which secured the end of the chain.

"I telt ye , he would' na herm ye", He slurred still obviously much under the influence of alcohol. My furious retorts did have some impact on his beer-sodden brain and he muttered apologies.

"You are off the list." I shouted, "Do not expect me ever to see you again. You have a new coat to pay for. I'm off." Belatedly he tried to make amends.

"I'll pay fer it. It wis a mistake, A only need a sustificate." He entreated.

"You will get no more certificates from me. Get back to work," I responded angrily, stalking out of the house, holding my button-less coat together and facing the rest of the call-round, ill-clad on a cold, wintry morning in the under- jacket.

Tommy may have been aware that I never put patients off my list and he was not going to be the exception. I made no moves against him. Time passed, there were few spurious calls for visits to him and I had all but forgotten the unfortunate event. After a surgery session one day Audrey, a new receptionist mentioned that, there was a brown paper parcel awaiting my attention and the contents were slopping around inside. Doctors and nurses approach such bottles with care, for patients, advised to provide a few millilitres of urine sample are wont to provide a litre of fluid, held in all sizes and types of bottle. This one however appeared sealed and a product of a famous whisky distillery. An unexpected gift, I quizzed Audrey about its source, but she could not recollect who had handed it in. Savouring the thought that I had one grateful patient, the contents aided relaxation after fraught days of labour.

Many months later, a midnight call came in from Tommy and I made my way grudgingly to his house. Mindful of my encounter with the dog, I wakened the neighbourhood with repeated banging on his door, resisting entreaties to enter, until he finally appeared at the entry. His chronic bronchitis had become much worse and the house call request merited attention.

"Ye need nae be feart. The dug's awa." He assured me retreating to his bed. As I examined him I reminded him that he still owed me for repair of a coat.

"But I made it up with ye," he remonstrated." I gied ye a bottle o' Black label."

"Whisky?" I queried dubiously, ready to deny such recompense.

"Aye" he said, I had a win racing the whippets and I gied ye a bottle which I left at the surgery."

"Wrapped in brown paper." I questioned.

"Aye."he responded," A didna forget ye and ye shared ma winnins." Somewhat chastened, I asked about the Alsatian.

"The brute bit me and it's gone to its maker." He answered. He had indeed made amends. To my amusement he then said,

"Can I have a self-inflicted sick sustificate?" a request which seemed to aptly label his health status. Remarkably, the dog incident had modified his behaviour and his inappropriate house calls had almost ceased, until unwarranted demands were terminated with his premature death from liver cirrhosis.

An Unexpected Bequest

I met many dogs on patient visits and most were friendly. I had my favourites. One old lady had a rough-haired female Jack Russell terrier which she had rescued from the dog-pound. Mistreated by the previous owner it lived a pampered life with her.

She became bed-bound and the terrier, ensconced on the bed, guarded her owner zealously. She rarely left her position except for a quick dash outside to answer the call of nature and back she would go to a protective stance on the bed. Over-fed and without exercise, her girth increased and she became a corpulent little sentinel.

I had attended Mrs Leitch her mistress for many years and latterly failed to appreciate her slow decline with the passage of time. She was always cheerful, never complained. I was aware that she had few visitors, led a lonely existence and the dog was a sole, inseparable companion. She liked a glass of sherry. It became a ritual for me to make her the last visit of the day, when a welcoming glass was waiting for me also. One day, she confided,

"I am ready to meet my maker, but I am very worried about the little dog. I do not want to have her put down or sent to an unwelcome home." Perhaps influenced by the beverage and erroneously anticipating that her end was not in sight, the dog was also very old and likely to die before her, I ebulliently stated,

"Oh, you still have time on your side. I will see to your dog and give it a good home". This was an unwise prognostication. A month later a police-women arrived at our home early one Sunday morning.

"I believe this is yours." She said and handed over the furry bundle in her arms.

"Mrs. Leitch died last night and the instructions by her bedside were that you were to care for the dog."

Taken aback and unprepared for a rebuttal, I accepted the terrier, which responded enthusiastically by licking my face. Hirta, my own Shetland collie, appeared and was immediately put to rout by an animal half his size. In minutes, the terrier established her status within our household. Although canine companions for many years, there was never further question about canine hierarchy. She was top dog.

Ann, my tolerant wife queried her name.

"Jess" I recalled, and she responded happily to the call of Jess for a month until I discovered the name on her collar was Gem. Friendly and captivating, she was very adaptable. Arriving as a rotund old lady accustomed to days of sloth and leisure she was thrown into the Sheltie's daily schedule of long walks, and weekend mountain climbs. These activities brought her weight down dramatically. She was soon as active as the collie and proved herself fearless. She would throw herself at a mini-cliff and battle to the top, while the collie found an easy route round. Streams were no obstacle and she threw herself into the torrent while the collie disdained to get his feet wet. Her fearlessness could create a problem compounded by her deafness, for she often failed to hear a recall whistle when she was foraging afield.

One May morning on a weekend break, when I was walking the dogs near the 1000 metre summit of Ben Chonzie, in the Southern Highlands, she chased after a mountain hare which had bolted close to her. The pursuit was fast and furious and within seconds she was out of sight. I scoured the summit for several hours to retrieve her, but finally had to leave the snow-clad summit and return to a disconsolate family. It was viciously cold, with snow flurries savaging the high tops. There seemed little chance that she would survive in this hostile environment. I advised the local police of the loss, with scant hope of her recovery. She had gone astray several miles from human habitation and a vast range of uninhabited moor and mountain surrounded her last sighting.

Hirta and family missed her company, but with the passing hours became reconciled to her permanent passing. A telephone call then came from the police in a village many miles from our climb. We are holding an ancient terrier which seems to be yours. Joyous at the news we hastened to rendezvous with our errant walking companion. She had been retrieved from a local shepherd in a nearby glen. The village policeman recounted the tale.

"A hill-walker was sitting having a sandwich near the summit of the Ben early this morning. A wet nose pushed between his hands and your dog wolfed down a purloined piece of bread. She was the lucky one. The weather has broken and there is now a blizzard blowing over the tops."

Our terrier had found haven in the nick of time for the gales blew on for several days covering the mountains in deep snow. She had apparently spent two nights exposed to temperature extremes until her salvation. The walker had put her in his rucksack and carried her down to a shepherd's shieling. A once cosseted, pampered pet, accustomed to the warmth of the bed room and bed had shown, remarkable resilience. She had escaped impounding twice and been tested by the rigours of nature and was none the worse for her experiences.

Concerned about her well-being we visited the vet. He examined her and wrote "of indeterminate age" on her record. Twelve or thirteen years old he guessed. Deaf and blind, she outlived the Shetland collie. Physically fit till her end, she was always game for a walk.In terminal decline she exhibited all the human features of dementia, as she wandered ceaselessly around the garden. With her ultimate demise, I could reminisce that while doctors were often left cash and valuables by grateful patients, I had been fortunate to be bequeathed a loyal four-legged friend of incomparable valour.

A Four-legged Saviour

A patient's dog once came to my rescue to my embarrassment. I had been out on a 1am. house visit and called into the surgery to use the telephone to check for other call requests during my absence. I normally left the car unlocked if I was only planning to be moments away, as streets were usually empty at that early hour. As I was alighting however, I noticed two drunk men, bottles in hand, sitting on a low stone wall in front of the next door property. One had an old retriever at his feet. I knew him to be Bobbie a local worthy, who reeled his way round the taverns in the town. With thoughts fixed on prompt return to a warm bed, I ignored them, entered the surgery, confirmed that there were no calls and thankfully returned to the car and prepared to start the engine.

The trouser pocket usually carrying the car keys was empty however and I searched through all my pockets with no result. Thinking I had left them on the surgery desk, I returned grudgingly to hunt for the errant keys. They were not there, not did a search round the car find them. My increasingly anxious activity held the interest of the drunks who were now on their feet, swaying synchronously above an alert dog which was not suffering from alcoholic overload. They were giggling away which added to my discomfiture. Desperately searching a failing memory to replay my route from car to telephone, I returned again to further search the surgery premises, with no result. Reconciled to the daunting prospect of ringing a sleeping wife to bring spare keys, I disconsolately returned again to the car.

This triggered a response from the watching trio. Bobbie, pulled wildly forward by the dog, was hauled to my side. I was in no mood for discourse with him and as he reeled closer a beery belch laced with bad breath and vomit engulfed me.

"Get out of my way."

He swayed before me in happy bonhomie as the dog bounded forward and sat down at my feet.

"Ye'll be busy the nicht." He slurred out with another blast of halitotic breath, which could have felled an ox, as I tried to avoid direct confrontation.

"I am busy, so get out of my way. " I retorted rudely.

"Ye'll nae be gaun far withoot they." He chortled, pointing at the dog..

She grasped in her mouth, the leather strap with my car keys. Furious rather than relieved I snarled,

"Where did she get them?"

"Auld Bess picked them up. Ye drapt them," he giggled.

In my haste I had apparently dropped them at the gate and the dog had retrieved them and brought them obediently to Bobbie. The drunken couple had enjoyed their little joke at my expense.

Thanks were perhaps in order but I irately berated him .

"You should have given them back to me right away."

"The dug wid nae gi them ti me," he defended himself. "She kent they wur no mine."

"She's got more sense than you, you're drunk," I stormed, coaxing the keys gently from Bess as she nudged her head towards me and offered a paw. I wondered at the life she led in his company as I returned gratefully to bed. The pair were regular sights about the town and I always enticed Bess over for a pat when meeting them. A large friendly animal she guarded her master in his inebriated travels between pubs and saved him from many an encounter with dangerous traffic.

Coping with Adversity

I was writing up my calls in the home-visit diary, when Bette, the receptionist, phoned to advise that, "Mrs .Young from Fern Bank asked if you would look in when you were passing."

My thoughts turned to a couple who were always a pleasure to meet. Callum was a quiet man who spoke with the sibilant lilt of the Scottish Highlander. He had been a local lawyer until retirement. Molly his long-time wife was buxom, but sprightly for her years and devoted to her husband's care. She had been an art teacher and was invariably making embroidery squares for a quilt when I visited. She had considerable talent and had exhibited her masterpieces of quilt-work at international exhibitions. I was amazed at what she could create with needle and thread.

"It keeps me busy," she would aver and I wondered how she did find the time for her hobby as her husband's health declined. They lived in a big country house with beautiful views down the valley. I always enjoyed the opportunity to leave the urban scene for this rural retreat. In initial home consultations she adroitly fielded questions about his mental state.

"He is doing fine and I can manage him" she would assure me. "Maybe a wee listen to his heart and something for constipation?"

I would auscultate his chest, hear a stout normal heart action and check him over physically. He responded in monosyllables, but appropriately, and then lapsed into his characteristic smiling silence. Beguiled by her words, I ignored a growing suspicion that all was not well with his cognition. Examination complete, Molly hastened to provide a cup of tea and delicious girdle scones heavily laden with butter.

Callum continued to say little but responded happily to my regular administrations and I was slow to appreciate the measure of his organic brain disease. There was then no foreseeable cure for dementia and Alzheimer's disease gained scant mention in text books. Inexorably, a dementing process was taking its toll however. As his mind unravelled, his physique wasted away. He became gaunt, disoriented and wholly dependent upon her. Concerned only about his physical well-being, she coaxed him into eating lovingly-prepared delicacies. Several times, I broached the subject of his mental status, always to be rebuffed.

"He is fine and no bother to me" Mention of a consultant opinion, or transfer to hospital was immediately dismissed and caring siblings supported her stance. Prior to the advancement of psychogeriatric care, the only placement for him would have been the locked ward of a mental institution, a solution I was unwilling to contemplate.

Monthly visits became weekly ones and the inevitable decline continued in physique and intellect. He needed 24 hour nursing care which she insisted she could provide.

"He is no bother at all," she would insist. The tray of tea and scones was always awaiting and I got into the habit of dropping in to see Callum whenever passing their abode. In time however, I became concerned for both of them. She was losing weight,

"Just a pound or two Doctor and I could do without it," Molly would say. Her devoted nursing care was undoubtedly a physical challenge and drain on her strength.

She adamantly refused external nursing input for Callum. Failure in State and family support could often wreck the health of the primary carer of a dementing patient. I was anxious to prevent this outcome. No cajoling or brow-beating however would shift her from what she believed her marital duty to a man she had loved for sixty years. It was possible in such circumstances to certify the patient as mentally insane and have them committed to an institution but I, perhaps cowardly, shrank from this alternative

Her weight redistribution accentuated an already full bosom and with a pink complexion she remained a comely woman despite her years, an appearance which seemed to belie any serious health problem. My suggestions at tea-time for a check-up and some tests were always met with,

"I'm fine. Have another scone doctor".

Callum became incontinent and despite her heroic administrations, the occasional whiff of ammoniacal urine testified to his loss of control, but to this was added an unidentifiable odour of decaying flesh which hung about as she nursed him. Fearing body ulcers or a tumour, I diligently sought the cause, but her nursing devotion had ensured that he was without any untoward lesions. Yet, the subtly, sickly smell of decaying flesh seem to linger about him. My worries finally centred on her for she had gradually became more pale and wan.

Unwillingly, she allowed me to take samples of her blood, but robustly refused to permit a personal examination.

"Not as long as Callum needs me, "she stoutly argued and the family and I again deferred to her judgement.

The blood tests merely showed an iron deficiency anaemia requiring simple iron medication and further investigation was stymied by lack of permission.

"I have not been eating too well," she grudgingly admitted.

Defeated, I waited for Callum's demise. She continued to care for him like a baby until he finally faded away and was gone. After the funeral, she admitted to being,

"A wee thing tired and breathless. While you are here Doctor, maybe I need a check-up?" and I waited for the revelation.

Finally submitting to a medical examination, she doffed her loose-fitting blouse and I prepared to sound her chest with the stethoscope. It suddenly became obvious that her large bust was not the product of mammary enlargement, but a creation of cotton wool and wad- dressings. The smell of putrefying flesh became overpowering. The unidentified cause of the malodour was now obvious.

"Perhaps you should take a look", she muttered apologetically.

Layer after layer of blood-soaked, purulent dressings were peeled away to ultimately reveal a horrible, hand-sized, fungating, tumorous mass, which had all, but obliterated the breast. The vast cancer had eaten away tissues down to underlying muscle. Appalled at this revelation, I stuttered,

"How long have you had this?

"A wee while."

"Months? Years?" I added.

"Maybe a year or two", she contributed defensively, "but Callum needed me. I have been dressing it twice a day'.

"It takes a lot of padding!"

"A pharmacy stock" I observed sardonically. "Why did you not tell me?"

"Och, you would have put me into hospital and who would have looked after Callum? It wasn't sore to begin with. Just a wee ulcer."

I assumed that she must have wide, bodily-spread, secondary lesions from this rapacious tissue-destroying monster and searched for more evidence of cancer. Surprisingly and to my relief none was apparent. Pessimistically, I arranged an appointment with a surgeon, who was staggered by the size of the lesion, the largest such skin presentation he had seen. Cancerous metastases to other parts of the body seemed certain, but he advised that operative removal of the mass was in her best interest. She willingly acquiesced and underwent prompt and extensive excision of the offending tissue from her chest.

Molly responded well, returned home and reinstituted the tea and scones routine, when the daily round took me her way, providing incentive for a courtesy call. Once again pink- cheeked and full of figure, she gamely sought a breast-reconstruction despite an uncertain prognosis. In due course she regained her former figure, with surgical remodelling of skin excised from her abdomen and thighs. Weeks and years passed with no recurrence until a failing heart demanded further house-calls. She was now ninety years old and as I prepared to listen to her irregular heartbeat, she would coquettishly enquire,

"What do you think of my thighs? The surgeon said I had only a few weeks to live, but I have proved him wrong. You know when the old breast went wrong, sometimes when I was dressing the ulcer the blood would spout out and hit the wall. When the pain got bad, I used to have a wee dram."

I marvelled at her fortitude and stoicism and enduring commitment to her husband. Clinically she should have died from the cancer, but she continued to live on to very ripe old age. Delayed intervention had not brought premature death to ever-thereafter assail my clinical conscience.

The psychological reactions of patients to illness and impending mortality continued to surprise me. Annie, a much younger woman responded very differently to a similar cancer which invaded her breast. Slender, attractive and forty years old, she was living with a much younger partner and could not envisage a body image that was less than perfect. When given the diagnosis she refused to acknowledge its significance, or consider radio and chemotherapy with possible temporary hair loss.

"I do not need treatment and I am definitely not going to hospital for an operation." She repeatedly said defensively. She resolutely refused to contemplate surgery and breast disfigurement. As time passed she continued to steadfastly dispute the diagnosis and repudiated a gloomy prognosis, without therapeutic intervention.

"I can look after myself, I am in control," she vowed when I pressed her.

Anne resorted to herbal remedies and meditation. She did not return for follow-up appointments and refused home entry to the district nurse when she called. After many failed attempts to provide support, faced with self-denial and a total resistance to cooperation, she fell beneath the team's radar and was lost to follow-up.

The ultimate price for her failure to face reality was paid, when secondary cancer spread rapidly through her body bringing untimely death. My attempted intervention on this occasion was timely, with a successful response to early therapy likely. Misplaced pride and refusal to confront reality resulted in a potentially avoidable premature end to life. Two similar presentations had brought very different individual responses and disparate outcomes. I marvelled at human behaviour and the variable personal response to illness.

Folie a Deux

"The Benjamins are next," Bette announced and my Monday morning gloom lifted. I always enjoyed their visits. Both showed a friendly interest in my family, which changed the dynamic of the consultation. Despite my protestations, they invariably brought a small gift for the children, whose development they had followed with interest from our arrival in Riverside. Although the couple were in senescent decline with failing organs and diminishing ability, they exuded tranquillity and bonhomie. I sometimes felt that they were the therapists and I was the one to benefit from the consultation. They were listeners and givers in nature, generously giving time and thought to others, which brought respect from villagers.

They made few professional demands upon me. When their deteriorating health required additional clinical support, they were profuse in apologies for taking up my time and attention.

"There are so many others in greater need," Bess Benjamin would slip in quietly.

"We do not like to bother you Doctor," James would confirm.

Inevitably the conversation during surgery visits turned to his travels, with emphasis on World War Two anecdotes and sea-going experiences. He had served on destroyers on the notorious Arctic convoys and cruisers in Far East battles and been on the last ship to escape successfully after the Japanese capture of Singapore. In ensuing years, he had travelled extensively and enjoyed a life of adventure. His descriptive way with words conjured up visions of daring-do.

Bess had however never ventured far beyond Edinburgh, but enjoyed much vicarious pleasure from listening to her husband's past exploits.

"I remember when I was serving on the battleship HMS Barham off the Falklands," he would start. His tales transported me from the tedium of the office to visions of Antarctica and far distant seas. Over time, their minor clinical needs were overtaken by age-related physical deterioration as they reached their mid-eighties. The physical effects I could manage, but the psychological changes in Bess were difficult to deal with. They were a devoted couple and James minimised her problems and gave unstinting attention his wife.

A childless couple they had entered old age without a supporting family.

"We can manage and the neighbours are helpful," James would state. Independent to a fault, they long-resisted community efforts to offer support, until the inevitable crisis arose. Even then, they questioned the need for sheltered housing, or a care home. Although eccentric in behaviour, they were held in high regard by neighbours who turned to them for sage counselling when times were hard.

Bess had come from an upper class environment, her father a successful businessman. She had lived as a spinster for many years with the widowed mother cared for by servants and had never learned to cook, or manage a household. She had never travelled far from Riverside. He had encouraged her dependence upon him and carried out daily chores. Her dependence increased, when she developed glaucoma and despite successful operations to her eyes, maintained that she was now blind. Consciously, or sub-consciously, this was an attention-seeking device. She received ever more help in activities of daily living from a willing husband. She refused to utilise talking-books and visual aids and James spent hours reading the content of books to her.

"Tell me about your time in the South China Seas," she would request and he would be off on a trip down memory lane.

She developed other obsessive traits, with fixed ideas about personal cleanliness, adopting rituals of hand-cleaning which left her hands chafed and raw. Communicating-room doors had to be left ajar and she could only use the toilet with James guarding a partially-closed door. Incongruously, she could travel locally in cars and public transport with equanimity and despite her hysterical blindness, could observe something of the passing scene.

Her dependent behaviour inconvenienced only her husband, who tolerated her whims with great forbearance, accepting the onerous demands of a functionally-fit wife. He kept their small bungalow ship-shape for a long time, but his physical decline accelerated. A failing heart reduced his strength and ability. He developed a rodent ulcer - a precancerous growth -in the corner of an eye, but refused to contemplate surgery or radiotherapy.

"It's not a problem," he insisted," at my age what difference does it make?"

I was inclined to agree with him, as it seemed likely that the growth would not be fatal and that his heart and lungs would give out before the growth became malignant. Hidden behind dark spectacles, the small tumour was not obvious and as they never made house call requests, there was no routine clinical surveillance. The hospital specialist failed to organise routine follow-up. Gradually their home environment deteriorated. Once spic and span rooms accumulated rubbish and living conditions became more squalid. Although charming to social workers concerned about their welfare, they resisted any external input and community support.

"We can manage," they assured Health Visitors who were powerless to intervene, until arthritis crippled James and he was forced to ask for house visits. They were now living and sleeping downstairs in squalor. Bureaucratic intervention was now obligatory and I made an assessment call. The once commodious hall was cluttered with piles of clothing and discarded packages, Indian carpets were clogged with refuse and strewn with papers. I edged into a living room, with space only round the two large extending arm chairs where the couple reclined by day and night.All around was the detritus accumulated over months of precarious survival and the grime of time. There was a stale smell of urine and putrification and both were gaunt and uncared for. I was appalled at the deterioration in them and their lifetime home. Their needs had failed to trigger an appropriate social work response. The time had passed for social rehousing, but care home accommodation was difficult to acquire.

I determined to short-circuit the conventional approach through the health visitor and rang the social-work department. Relations between family doctors and social workers were often strained and with their superiors always fractious. Bosses always appeared as bureaucratic, inflexible form-fillers. Patient's clinical needs took less priority with them than 'needs assessments' which often took weeks to organise, with further delay in report-back. The report usually acknowledged the need, outlined the services required and advised.

"There is neither funding nor staff to meet the demand."

"Mr. Bullock" I requested. Fred Bullock was an obese, florid man with a high opinion of his personal status and skills. We had intermittently done battle over the years, when he had refused to consider my pleas for assistance for patients whose needs seemed urgent. He loved his rigid, inflexible systems and made his social work staff adhere closely to regulations, with no place for special cases.

"Can you help with two of my patients?" as I presented my case for urgent attention. In this instance Fred was again unmoved by my pleading and adamant that the conventional assessment process was followed.

"We have many clients to consider," he averred, his words confirming that ill people for him were mere documents and data.

"Office bureaucrat," I shouted voicing my ire and slammed down the telephone abruptly before setting off to revisit the couple.

On arrival James shouted, "Come in." He looked anaemic and she was losing weight. I checked his blood and found he was deficient in red cells and iron.

"What do you get to eat?" I demanded.

"Oh, the baker and milk man are very good and call to the door. We get by." James said stoically.

"What is in your meals?"

"We have pies and rolls and a tart or two," he responded. This was in fact their main sustenance.

"It's a home–help for you, or hospital. If hospital, Bess will have to go into a home on her own." Fearing change they both resisted leaving their home and temporary help was arranged.

"We can manage, we can manage." James protested. His resistance was finally overcome when the inevitable crisis arose.

Two men proclaiming themselves to be council-support workers arrived at the house. They conned their way into the living room and made off with a substantial amount of money from the home. Bess chatted with them as, behind her back, they rifled contents of the bureau, which sat behind the door, as her husband was distracted. James later admitted to keeping sizeable amounts of money scattered about the house. He had a distrust of banks and latterly had been unfit to visit a branch.

The Benjamin's now grudgingly accepted visits from Jessie, a hard-working home-help, who removed some of the accumulated filth. The Health Visitor then reported that Jessie's time with them was being directed to acquiring more pies, pastries and meals which did not require cooking. Their living milieu had been reduced to the one room, where they were sleeping in arm chairs. Bess's heart began to fail and she developed grossly swollen legs. Both were incapable of personal care, but were still disputing the need to leave their home of sixty years.

A place was ultimately found for them in the only available local care home. On my first visit, the room they shared was garlanded with floral bouquets from villagers but, with the passage of time, local memories of the couple dimmed. They had few visitors and the flowers disappeared. Only photographs and souvenirs of ancient naval ships and foreign travel perched on the window-ledge, were reminders of his adventurous past. Bessie and James shrunk in physique as they became totally dependent on care staff.

The expansion of the skin tumour slowly ruined his sight and he could no longer read to Bess. They sat much of the time hand in hand, as he recounted memories of his days in the navy. They were neglected by an uncaring staff and a crooked establishment owner fraudulently misappropriated their savings, until they were left destitute. This, the final ignominy compounded their mental and physical disintegration. On my final visit, there was silence in the room as he sat by the bedside holding her hand.

Sightless, James acknowledged my presence, but Bess seemed semi-conscious and did not respond.

He was courteous as always.

"It's kind of you to call Dr.Welman when you have so many others to see. I have something for you" and he indicated a small parcel. I hope they will give you some pleasure. Then all was quiet for some minutes until he said quietly,

"She is finished,"in a lugubrious monotone. The statement reflected my own opinion, but one I was not about to express. I said nothing. Then came a tremulous whisper from Bess,

"I am not away yet!"

Her last words, she died shortly after. Devoted to her to the end, his own demise soon followed. The parcel contained books on Arctic convoys and the fall of Singapore in World War Two and a set of medals for valour. Always modest he had never mentioned his decorations. The funeral was a reminder to villagers of happier days and their selfless ways and they responded en masse. An unassuming couple had won a place in public affection by their selfless devotion of time and interest to others.

Colourful Personalities

Consultations in general practice in far-off days lasted on average five minutes. This through-put, depended on speedy diagnosis, decision making and management. In reality, consultations nearly always overran and patient "no-shows" were relied upon to keep approximately to booked appointment times. Generally, patients got the time needed to deal with their problem, which meant that many patients waited long past their appointed time-slot,

Emergency house calls and urgent patient demands impinged heavily on this gruelling consulting schedule and "heart-sink" patients – regular attenders with chronic conditions defying current medical expertise – further distorted endeavours to stick rigidly to allotted management times. Unannounced, urgent requests to receptionists, from worthies with colourful personalities, could create mayhem and leave staff, doctors and conventional patients inconvenienced.

One such interruption guaranteed maximal upset to management routines on her rare appearances. Agnes's presence never needed to be announced. On arrival, a smell of wood-smoke, body odour, unwashed skin and clothing pervaded the waiting room and escaped into the surroundings. Other patients, suddenly aware of her presence, backed away and moved to distant seats. They were relieved when called for consultation, while she remained blissfully unaware of her anti-social impact. Receptionists tried unobtrusively to combat the inescapable stench emanating from her proximity, with frantic puffs of air freshener, patently unfit for task. They contrived to expedite her prompt departure, while she would happily endeavour to engage with her trapped neighbours, addressing them in a broad Scots dialect few could interpret. Invariably, a knock would come on my surgery door.

"Could you possibly take a patient early?" from a receptionist making an urgent request for Agnes's immediate consultation. She was always seen before her turn, priority attention never disputed by the most belligerent of waiting patients. She would bound into the consulting room full of bonhomie,

"Hi Doc," she would shout conversing in a thick Aberdeenshire brogue, testimony to her native tongue. She was not a regular list-patient despite the familiarity, but an itinerant vagrant of no fixed abode, who appeared at the time of berry and potato harvesting. NHS administrators disliked this categorisation and insisted she provided a temporary address. When pressed with this demand, Agnes would evasively offer, "The Fox Wood," and proffer "The Den," when asked for house name or number. Medical records sent to this venue exasperated the local postman, for Agnes slept rough under the stars, deep within the confines of a patch of woodland.

Weather-beaten of visage and coarse in feature, her wearing apparel remained unchanged irrespective of season. She wore scuffed, knee-high rubber Wellington boots, thick red woollen tights, a mud-spattered skirt, tattered hole-ridden jersey and an even more disreputable cardigan. Her only provision for inclement weather in winter was a many-pocketed camouflaged anorak. Only once did she deviate from this norm. She swept in, enveloped in a scarlet cloak rescued from a skip, which trailed more on the ground than over her. Appearing like an ancient crone in a red riding hood and only lacking a broom-stick, she startled neighbourhood children meeting her in the dusk.

"I've brought you a bite." She would burst out, full of goodwill. The spacious pockets of her anorak often held a rabbit or pheasant, with the carcase adding to the smells wafting from her person. The mutilated carcase was proffered in return for my services, for she appreciated my therapeutic efforts. Adept with wire-snares and animal-traps, her catches complemented a basic diet of herbs and vegetables lifted from fields, augmented by a high alcohol intake. Nancy was a binge-drinker. When she received a wage, it was spent promptly in the nearest public-house and she was regularly seen reeling through the town late on Saturday nights. Always benign and cheerful, the police would move her on and she would sleep off the alcoholic stupor in her lair in Fox Wood.

She invariably sought medication for a "sair chest and wheeze.

"While a'm here, a need somethin' for my kist, "she would cajole. Her chronic bronchitis was aggravated by a smoking habit and year-round living out of doors with little shelter. "It helps keeps the cauld oot." She would state dismissively when I criticised her addiction. She often resorted to pipe-smoking her tobacco, enjoyed a cheroot and occasionally, when temporarily affluent, would offer me a choice cigar! She scorned state welfare support, revealed little of her past and was scathing about going "on the brew," her description of the Benefit Office. Intelligent and remarkably well read, she always clutched a paperback book-often a classic novel-in her wanderings, but she refused to sign up for State aid. She gave the impression that she had come from a wealthy family and believed that others had greater need of state and medical support.

"I can look efter m'sel," she would remonstrate, when I suggested institutional assistance. "Am nae gaun to ony pair hoose. Ithers need it mair than me."

She criss-crossed Scotland howing turnips and swedes, picking berries, stalk-cleaning roses, potato-gathering, stacking hay and mucking-out byres. She loved the outdoors, walked miles in all weather and was enviably independent. With her worldly possessions stowed in an old battered children's perambulator, she jaunted between work-sites oblivious to the diversion she often forced upon passing traffic.

Despite the accompanying malodour, I enjoyed her visits, although she always over-ran her allotted consultation time. Staff insisted on fumigating the surgery after her departure, otherwise an olfactory reminder of her visit would linger for days. She was a living legend, with an endless fund of couthy, country tales drawn from rugged experience. She had a rumbustious sense of humour and raucous laugh and cackled noisily at her own jokes. On one of her visits I made her day. Living close to the wild, she was very observant, an attribute not matched with tactfulness.

"Yer minds gaun Doc." She burst out with a great laugh and prolonged giggle. I was at a loss as to the cause of her unexpected remark. Rendered almost speechless in her mirth, she pointed at my feet and continued with a guffaw which penetrated to the waiting room.

"See yer shin" she spluttered out.

I looked downward, dismayed to see that I was wearing shoes of different colour. I had been called out during the night to a cardiac asthma case, which had kept me busy until the start of surgery. Dressing in the dark by my bedside, I had mistakenly slipped on an unmatched pair of shoes and progressed in due course, straight from the heart patient to the first morning consultation, unaware of this eccentricity. When consulting, I usually swung my chair round to face patients and my shoe-wear must have been prominently displayed to consulting patients through the morning. Tactfully, no one had drawn attention to the anomaly until her arrival. She thought this a great joke. I could hear her cackling away, regaling my misfortune loudly to occupants of the waiting-room as she left the premises. I spent the rest of the surgery session with feet well hidden beneath the desk and ignoring the amusement of staff apprised of my discomfort by Agnes's jocular remarks.

Agnes never forgot this little episode and would often greet me thereafter with,

"Aye, Yer right weel dressed the day Doc" looking pointedly at my feet with a lusty chuckle..

In time she met a male soul-mate Dougall, a local" ne'er do well," who joined her on her pub crawls and syphoned off her hard-won earnings. He had a shock of unruly hair, which stuck out in all directions from under disreputable deer-stalker headwear he called his "comin' and gaun" hat. His trousers were held up with a waist-loop of binder twine and his multi-layered, hole-strewn jerseys were liberally endowed with bits of straw.

The pair took to attending the surgery together. As unkempt in appearance as she, he invariably smelled of whisky and stale vomit and confined himself to the waiting room, which he soon had to himself. When questioned he always responded,

"Am wi' Nessie," and resisted staff encouragement to wait outside. Other patients decided their ailments could wait for another day.

Left alone, on a rare day of unimpaired cognition prior to Christmas, he saw an opportunity to make a few free acquisitions. A local artist had been invited to hang some paintings on the waiting-room walls in the hope of making sales to waiting patients. Dougall surreptitiously stole them all and disappeared for a few months. They were never seen again, but the resultant insurance compensation delighted the artist. It was tempting to think that he had displayed his ill-gotten gains on the walls of his reported abode –"the Cliffs".

After a decade of Agnes's unannounced visits, her reappearance was much overdue after a particularly harsh winter. Dougall also had not been seen about the town. Discreet enquiries to the police brought no information of the vagabonds' whereabouts. They inferred a drop in work-load at pub closing-times in their absence. Receptionists discontinued stocking room fresheners and my consultations resumed humdrum normality.

Much later, a paragraph in the local newspaper recorded the demise of a local worthy in a road traffic accident. Dougall's drunken exploits had been finally terminated. Many months went by, with no further visits from Agnes. I forgot about her, until I found myself one wintry morning on a country walk leading high above the cliffs abutting Fox Wood. The pair of miscreants came to mind. On impulse, I climbed down the rock-fall into the inner recesses of the wood, on a course soon regretted.

The sanctuary was a tangle of dead briars, matted bracken, fallen branches and hidden boulders. Forward progress was slow and dangerous. Repeated back-tracking was forced by the intrusion of massive boulders. I soon lost direction. Pathless, the wood was almost impenetrable. I was therefore surprised to come upon a patch of flapping, green fabric almost wholly hidden by tree debris of past seasons.

On closer inspection, it was revealed as an ancient, tattered bivouac tent.

There was no sign of an inhabitant, scant evidence of path-entry and I was minded to pass by. Then I stumbled over some rusted tubular steel. Pitched full-length in to the undergrowth, I saw that the obstacle was the handle on an old pram. With renewed interest, I viewed the partly-collapsed tent and tentatively heaved it erect. The front door partially opened as it regained its shape. In the interior, I glimpsed a bundle of mouldy, sodden old clothing. Turning it over with a stick, I was taken aback to find that it consisted of a torn cardigan and a black bordered, bedraggled, crimson cloak. There was also a filthy primus-stove, some cooking implements and mildewed paper back books, but otherwise the retreat was empty

Had I discovered Agnes's bolt-hole in Fox Wood. If so what had happened to her? Had she moved on, become ill, been accosted? Dismayed at the possibility that her earthy remains might be unattended nearby, I made a peremptory search of the vicinity and the police a more thorough investigation thereafter. They widened their enquiries, but Agnes had disappeared from human ken. She had apparently left this earth with none to grieve her passing. A colourful character had left the patient list. Humdrum surgery consultations were no longer enlivened by her eccentric appearance and the local scene was the poorer for the demise of two colourful personalities.

A Conniving Rogue

Another personality also made a considerable impact on the practice but she and her tribe did little to brighten our day. They added considerably to the burden of general practice and were skilled at using the health service to their maximal advantage.

Maddy Milligan was a, well-endowed, peroxide-blonde-haired woman of thirty-odd years. A tiny figure less than five feet high her stature concealed a scheming, malign personality. The benign appearance belied her antisocial behaviour, which would plague practice partners and me for years. A con merchant par excellence, she arrived in surgery one day to dolefully explain, that she had just arrived in the area from Glasgow, with her husband.

"He is dying of cancer and is in great pain. He needs pain-killers. He is so brave."

"What pain-killers? I questioned.

"Strong ones," she replied. "His last doctor gave him....." and she named a morphine derivative. Her, soulful performance was impressive, but I initially resisted her request. In the absence of a corroborative letter from her past GP, I was unwilling to prescribe addictive medication. She gave a lucid account of his medical history, therapies and drug doses however.

Clinical notes can take weeks to circulate between practices. The heart moving account of her husband's distress induced me to give her the benefit of the doubt and sufficient tablets to last over the weekend. My partners were equally gullible. Without my knowledge, she rotated round them, accumulating a hoard of strong analgesic and dangerous drugs. She then astutely worked her way round all the area doctors over coming weeks, conning each and every one, until her subterfuges were discovered. She had divorced her husband years ago and was now making a lucrative living, acquiring addictive drugs in his name and selling them.

Maddy's name was removed from all the local practice-lists and no doctor would willingly accept her as a patient. NHS. Authorities, with a legal responsibility to provide medical services to every citizen, had to step in and allocate her to a GP. This was the start of a 'merry-go-round' as she was allocated to an unwilling doctor, who often responded immediately by removing her from his list. Finally, local doctors agreed to accept her and her extended family- all thieves, junkies or drug dealers- for three months at a time. Thereafter, after 12 weeks and a day she was then allocated to another doctor, to obfuscate her way through another professional relationship. An inveterate liar incapable of adhering to the truth, she and her large family of children, grand-children, aunts and uncles were dominated by wee Maddie, she had inculcated them into criminal ways.

They took advantage of all the benefits provided by a benevolent welfare state, acquiring privileges and assuming none of the associated responsibilities. None of them worked, most were drug-addicted and many spent lengthy sojourns in prison. They made high demands on the State Health Service, which they treated with scant regard. Calls for medical care were always urgent, requiring immediate attention and usually made out of conventional working hours. Favoured requests for a doctor's attention for "the wean" arrived about midnight, at a time when I longed for sleep and a respite from patient demands.

"It's Maddy here, A want the doctor." She would shout on the telephone. At a time when patients were always addressed with the prefix Mr. or Mrs. she was the notorious exception . Her nickname was scrawled across her record in red ink, in a warning to locums and trainees of trouble to come.

"A want the doctor the noo," was her usual out of hours demand, "The wean's no weel." Any endeavour on my part to avoid a visit was met with invective, abuse and aggression.

"We'll dae ye up. Ye'll get a batterin',"the family would threaten. Each call provided just enough misleading information, from a tribe fully conversant with medical parlance, to infer that the condition described might be serious and merit a house call. It never was! The underlying motive was the perceived need for a cough bottle, stomach-settler or sedative, dispensed promptly by the doctor at their convenience, to save them a conventional visit to surgery and pharmacy.

"The bairn's got a split heid. Ye'll need to come doon," she announced on one occasion. Anticipating a child with an axe injury to the head, I hastened to the house to do some stitching. On arrival the bairn was romping round the floor and Maddie had engineered another inappropriate house visit. She defended herself noisily and with cunning,

"Ye're gittin deef. A said a splittin' heid, no a split heid!" and I remembered belatedly that in the local vernacular, a "splitting head" was a headache.

The many daughters in the family never married, but had a series of semi-permanent relationships usually ending whenever another pregnancy was forthcoming. Mothers were not always aware of the child's parental surname and often a three year old would pipe up as I was writing their prescription, "I'm no; a Johnson, I'm a Wilson. Ma faither's rid Jock".

The children would watch television until after midnight, when they were given fish and chips, before bedtime in the small hours of the morning. They were left to their own resources through much of the day, but were invariably well-dressed, as parents stole clothing from local stores. One enterprising 'mum-to-be' even acquired a high quality baby buggy for her new-born by wheeling a new one out from the store, circumnavigating the check-out. As single parents on benefit, most had their own flats, always well-stocked with stolen goods.

Wee Maddy lived in a long tenement block in Haughside. A caring town council had built a wooden fence round neighbouring small frontal gardens, which many residents then used as runs to keep ferrets, rabbits, greyhounds, or totally neglected. Most of the wood fences disappeared into residents' fires during the ensuing winter. The council reacted by building replacement steel railings, which lasted a little longer, but were soon distorted and sagging after use as vaulting bars by local youths.

Her abode was immediately recognisable. Within the confines of the garden were old newspapers, junk, cardboard discards and rubbish, a foot or more high. The content of the garden varied with the season for high winter winds lifted the papers over the rails, to scatter them round the neighbourhood. The urban fox and local dogs regularly feasted on abandoned food cartons. Inside the place however was always immaculate. She took pride in showing off the latest TV or high-fi equipment nefariously acquired by the family. Her behaviour was eccentric and she was wont to interrupt the clinical consultation, throw open a window and deposit rubbish to the pile below.

"While ye'er here, a need mair o' the bottle for the bairn." was the start of many a consultation and she would then adroitly work her way round to demands for pain killers.

"Ma backs killin' me. A need mair pain-killers," she would ultimately demand.

"A canna sleep at night and need sleeping pills," with voice rising in volume if her wishes were resisted,so neighbours could hear her impassioned pleas. She would then begin to curse and malign my resistant response. Some partners intimidated by threats of,

"Oor Jock will dae ye up," would take the line of least resistance and grudgingly give her a few analgesics and sedatives. She was very keen on one particular pain killer then on wide prescription.

"At least gie me some "Dae Guid" pills," she would wheedle. A proprietary medicine, it had the initials of the drug company on the tablet. The DG convinced many of our patients that this was a potent medicine. In time we discovered that she was mixing the product with hard drugs and selling the concoction. Established GPs. refused to supply her with medication. She cunningly took advantage of locums and emergency doctors to maintain her black-market drug stocks.

The local constabulary had regular run-ins with wee, but mighty Maddy who demonstrated a readiness to throw anything at hand, at offending members of the force. Many members of the extended family were doughty characters feared by more puny policemen and women. PC Duguid, in a moment of weakness, revealed that, he would opt for the hazards of policing a Rangers versus Celtic football match rather than face Maddy and her clan. Police officers deployed in teams rather than pairs when dealing with them.

Out of fear or respect, the family had a considerable following in the community. Columns of the Harborough Gazette would have been thinner without weekly reports of their household demeanours. One son was arrested for drug addiction and sentenced, despite an outcry from Maddy and her supporters.

She started a campaign condemning the drug-pushers who she said had led her son astray. Supported by a few vocal supporters her protest created ripples and the local newspaper embraced her cause. Soon this reached the national press, with Maddy portrayed as warrior-saint and campaigner intent on ridding the nation of drug addiction. To her delight, do-gooders sent her donations. She had won herself recognition and funds.

One April Fool's day, a reporter in the Harborough Gazette saw the opportunity for a prank, which rocked the composure of affluent citizens of the town. The newspaper announced dramatically,

"Local campaigner wins millions," and in smaller print, "Maddy wins million pounds on lottery. Will buy house in River View." The location was in a highly desirable and posh local residential area. Residents of this salubrious and affluent district were appalled at this revelation. Fearing a fall in land values and the prospect of the wee terror and accompanying clan as next door neighbours many made anxious, confirmatory calls to the newspaper office..

Respite from her unwanted practice intrusions finally came when the full weight of the Law caught up with her. She had attracted some notoriety and brought an unwelcome spotlight on the local police force. Assiduously detective Jimmie and his team accumulated enough evidence to establish she was a drug-dealer plying an active trade both near and far. Arrested, the clan made noisy protests during criminal proceedings, but at last her criminal activities brought retribution. She was sent to prison for several years, exchanging the recidivist comforts of her home for a cell, where she no longer could toss rubbish from the window. Rumour had it that, with her devious talents she was still dealing drugs in her new environment.

The incarceration finally took her name permanently off practice lists. Late evenings were no longer invaded by her screams of profanity when there was resistance to her demand for a house call. She ultimately died while incarcerated. The clan turned out en masse at her funeral, many of them handcuffed to prison officers.

Drug addicts became an increasing problem in the nineties. I had several injecting adult patients who had ruined their hands and arms with self-injections. The constant attack on veins ultimately destroyed them and caused nerve damage to hands and fingers. Many had several amputated fingers. Despite the self-inflicted injury, they would continue to self-abuse until they finally killed themselves. The addiction forced them into crime to support their craving for banned drugs. They were all skilled confidence tricksters manipulating the health service in efforts to acquire prescribed and state-controlled dangerous drugs.

A Druggie

O'Connor was one of these. He would, lie, cheat and steal to get narcotic drugs and was a dangerous man when deprived of drugs to fuel his addiction. The threat of violence overhung each consultation if his intimidating demands were not met. Unkempt and gaunt in appearance, he had only part use of his left arm which was palsied from repeated venous injections and two fingers and a thumb on his right hand He was usually under the influence of his addiction and always belligerent. Treatment programmes rationed his drug medication and the regimen never satisfied his needs.

"Gie me ma injection, or I'll knife you," was no empty threat, despite his disablement, when I was sitting alone in the surgery building, late in the evening. Hung-over with heroin, he was scarcely in command of his actions. As he sat between me and the door, the only means of escape, these consultations could be intimidating. Refused treatment, he and other junkies resorted to devious wiles to fuel their drug-craving.

On one occasion, Joe Hall the local pharmacist interrupted my consultation enquiring about a script I had recently written. I recalled writing it for a few potent analgesic tablets an hour before and reassured him that it was a bona fide prescription.

"You had better come and see it." He advised. "The patient is still here. I do not think it has your signature." Reluctantly I left a busy surgery session and sped round to the pharmacy, to discover that the patient had departed without his requested script. I looked at the signature and said,

"It's mine." and declared that it was indeed a controlled drug provided by me within the terms of O'Connor's rehabilitation programme.

"I disagree." said Joe, an experienced chemist who had been dispensing my prescriptions for years. "This is not your writing." I had another look and remained unconvinced. My signature, like my writing, was often a hurried scrawl.

"I am getting the police to look at this ", he said as I returned to the waiting patients.

A few days later, I was called to the local police station by John Swale the detective on the fraud team. "I want you to look at some scripts." he said offering me a small pile of prescriptions written on a partner's prescription pad. All of them purported to be signed by me. On this occasion, I could confirm that although the signature looked like mine, I had not written the details of the addictive dangerous drugs, which had been prescribed, all to the same person. I disclaimed writing them.

"These are not mine." and he said,

"Come and have a look at this doc."

He led me to a microscope under which lay the script submitted by my chemist friend. I could view the enlarged signature and it was apparent that it had been created by carefully drawn, joined-up small lines and was a forgery. It had in fact been copied from an imprint. The prescriptions had been stolen from a partner and my signature had been copied on to fraudulent scripts. Only Joe's eagle eye had uncovered the fraud, which had been running successfully for several months. Criminals had been making the rounds of local chemists to obtain addictive drugs and then selling them on in a lucrative racket while it lasted.

A few weeks later, Bette my receptionist rushed excitedly in to the surgery.

"I have just seen a guy looking like your fraudster entering the chemist's shop across the road." PC Duguid responded to our call for aid. He cunningly awaited the miscreant's exit from the shop then literally collared him in possession of the drugs. A violently protesting O'Connor was arrested. Justice had finally caught up on leader and gang. His fraudulent and socially psychopathic reign finally came to an end with his death in prison. It had taken an astute and sharp-eyed pharmacist to recognise a fraudulent signature that I had claimed as my own.

Conniving rogues, benefit frauds and criminals created challenging incidents, to enliven the working day and brought some drama to tedious watches of the night

Distorted Perceptions

Harry was a patient for a short time. A single man living with his mother, he was podgy of build, slow moving, soft-spoken and reserved. Very committed to parish politics, he was often at odds with local authorities who resisted innovation. We met occasionally, as he owned an art shop and I bought painting materials from him. I made a few house calls to his home when he had influenza. He was always courteous, invariably helpful, but bland and reticent. He was keen on archery and gun sports. On a domiciliary visit on one occasion; he showed me guns kept legally in his home.

"Here Doc, get a feel of them. They handle well," and he lovingly handed me one of his pistols."

I gripped the weapons gingerly. My only previous experience with guns had been a Lee-Enfield rifle used on the rifle range during National Service in the RAF. This was not one of my innate skills for, to the fury of the gunnery sergeant, I regularly missed my target, but hit that of my neighbour.

"I practise once a week at the gun-club." he added. "You should have a go."

"I don't think so. Not my forte," I hurriedly replied.

Their future significance and fatal potential would take years to be revealed. A bit of a loner, Harry was supportive to the community and showed no obvious aberrant psychological or sexual tendencies. There was always a slight flattening of affect in his demeanour, however with a natural smile or laughter slightly repressed. It seemed that he could never quite respond with hearty laughter, or react spontaneously to sorrow, with overt grief. Small, with slicked-down, red hair, his facial expressions never quite matched, or reflected, the emotional content in his conversations.

He had a marked antagonism towards neighbourhood officials, which appeared justified to some extent, as I often also met with bureaucratic obstruction.

"They block all my suggestions and are always sending people to inspect my shop", he regularly complained. "I am going to get them," rather darkly more than once. This choice of words may have been a window into darker thoughts, but seemed figurative speech at the time.

"I am gunning for them." He did say once in regard to local officials, but the significance of the words escaped me. It was an expression I sometimes used myself, when confronted with destructive officialdom. Sometimes however his thinking process seemed obtuse but not markedly pathological. On our rare contacts I sometimes left him with a slight suspicion that his modus operandi was unconventional. There was much to admire however in his behaviour and community spirit. In time I lost touch with him, when he moved away from the practice. In retrospect his conduct seemed slightly eccentric but not all that different from other patients, some of whom had bizarre behavioural traits.

I was listening idly to the radio one morning several years later when an announcement was made,

"There has been a shooting incident at the labour exchange in Harborough."

A shooting tragedy unfolded. The gunman had taken several guns into the building and randomly shot at occupiers of the building, with several being killed. He had shot at officials and finally turned a weapon on himself and committed suicide.

Later I realised that the murderer had been Harry. The news report read,

"A gunman armed with guns and ammunition, entered the building. Wearing a mask and firing guns, he shot indiscriminately at people, then turned a gun on himself. The gunman, a firearms enthusiast, had licensed guns."

Complaints about his threatening conduct had previously led to police investigation which revealed no evidence of improper behaviour. He had recently sent a letter to the Queen complaining that he was being hounded by local authority officials for deeds he had not been responsible for. Proclaiming his innocence, he had requested Her Majesty to intervene on his behalf.

At the Public Enquiry, witness statements suggested he was paranoid, but the official report concluded that his actions on that day could not have been predicted. I found it difficult to accept that the mild mannered, easy-going young man of yester-year could have embarked on such a murderous expedition, with malevolent evil intent. His grossly disturbed state of mind was difficult to contemplate and the mental deviance hard to explain.

More details of his character came to light when in ensuing weeks PC Duguid came to see me as a patient. He had responded to an emergency call and been one of the first on the crime scene. The appalling scene of slaughter was etched in his memory and was disturbing his sleep. I remembered how keen he had been to be called to solve a murder but he had never anticipated a multiple tragedy.

Over several visits, he mentioned some of the past history of the gunman in the intervening years since our acquaintance, Harry's mother had died and he had lived alone. Bankrupt and unemployed, he made regular visits to Harborough Benefit and Employment Offices, where he had upset workers with his demands for work. He had developed paranoid delusions that he was being victimised and excluded from work, so much part of his life. Well known in the local community, no-one had detected the measure of his grievance against officials, the depth of his distorted perceptions and potential for grossly aberrant behaviour. He had never sought medical help and never been so antisocial as to attract serious investigation. Without criminal record, he had continued to enjoy access to weapons. This finally allowed him to perpetrate the murders of helpless office workers and local citizens.

In retrospect, there was nothing I could think of in his conduct in our professional or social relationship, to have prompted consideration that he might one day attempt mass murder. Easy gun access had made the killings possible. After several multiple shooting tragedies the ownership of hand guns was finally restricted in Britain.

Poetry and dementia

Mental disorders were always difficult conditions to deal with in general practice. Many mentally-ill people continued to live in the community as mental health resources and hospital accommodation was limited. Their unfortunate spouses and carers often had to cope with difficult behaviour which they managed by day. Night-time demands often had them recourse to medical aid in anti-social hours. House-call requests in the early morning hours were not uncommon but always unwelcome. Those that came in between 2 to 3 am dragged me from deep slumber into the harsh realities of the new day. Grudgingly, I would focus thoughts on the intrusion, hoping that the call could be deferred till conventional waking hours.

Only rarely however was one able to convince the caller that delay would be acceptable. In those early days of my career, patient relatives had to leave their own repose and home to venture into the street to find a telephone box. Although mobiles were an innovation of the future, later many people had a phone by the bedside. Snugly warm patients could demand attendance, without venturing from the comfort of bed.

Inevitably, I would leave the cosy matrimonial bed and in winter face sub-zero temperatures and a car whitely-festooned with frost and as cold as a morgue. Silently cursing the ethics of a profession that ensured much interrupted sleep, I would drive through deserted streets, often struggling to find a street and house name or number in unlit locations.

On one occasion I initially believed that escape from the call was possible.

"There are intruders in the house." came from a cultured female voice I did not recognise.

"Call the police" I responded with relief.

"They are Nazis" responded the voice with conviction. "They have come to take me to Bunchenwald!" My heart sank, as I suspected I was talking to a deluded personality.

"Go back to bed and they will go away," I suggested in a final effort to avoid a house call.

"You will have to come over doctor," a voice broke in, "It's Anderson from Faraway Cottage. She does not recognise me and has just attacked me with a carving knife."

Acknowledging the inevitable, I groped for out-door clothing and prepared for a lengthy outing to the aptly named cottage, which lay at the end of a long glen with no prospect of a quick return to bed. The house was situated at the top of a steep hill thinly-covered with ice, unvisited by the gritter truck, and I corkscrewed to the top in a series of uncontrolled slithers. A business-man I recognised waited at the door.

"James Anderson", as he introduced himself. "It's Elsie, doctor. We have been married for forty years and she does not recognise me."

He led me into a palatial bed-room where his wife was fluttering about in a floral negligee clutching a long curved knife.

"A man has been sleeping in my bed." she exclaimed conversationally, "He just gets in beside me." She was not overtly disturbed by this event, but her poor husband retreated smartly when she lunged at him with the knife when she again became aware of his presence.

"He is one of these Nazis." she continued flatly, "They have come to take me to Buchenwald."

"She was fine when she went to bed," exclaimed the husband sheltering behind me. "but now I do not know what to do with her." She is filling up note-books with scribbles and is very violent when I approach her."

At 3 am, neither did I. Psychiatrists and social workers did not acknowledge the need to visit clients in the middle of the night. From long experience, I was aware that a prolonged series of telephone calls to health professionals and ward staff now faced me. This would take up the remainder of the night. I half-heartedly tried to address her delusions and started a one-sided conversation. She listened intently then suddenly thrust several sheets of writing paper upon me.

She writes poetry explained her spouse. I glanced at the words which I expected to be mere gibberish. A second look had me realise that they were exceptional pieces of poetry from a cultured author.

"She is always scribbling," he added. "She did that while we were waiting for you." It appeared that I had a patient who had paranoid delusions and was either dementing or schizophrenic, but had retained cultural skills.

Jerry, one of my partners, had come to surgery one morning with a black eye after being accosted by an old man suffering from a dementing process, who had violently objected to being physically examined. I kept a wary eye on the knife as she agitatedly wandered about the room attempting to corner us.

After an hour spent in efforts to placate her, I finally managed to give her tranquillising medication, then organise further psychiatric care. The knife attack on the husband convinced an unwilling resident hospital doctor to admit her to a ward. There she struggled with increasing delusions and wrote ever more poetry most of considerable merit. Her solicitous husband ultimately managed to have the manuscript published. She had only started to write poems as the dementing process became apparent. Distortions of thought and moments of reality had given her a rare lucidity in poetic expression.

Driving back home in the new morning, I was reminded of my psychiatry oral test in Final Medical School Examinations. I was presented with an immaculately coiffured and dressed lady who spoke in a cultured Scottish accent, testimony to one-time domicile in Edinburgh's up-market New Town. As I took her clinical history, she spoke eloquently and convincingly of her time in India and occasions when she had met royalty. It was rare to get loquacious patients talking so sagaciously. Usually one was met with a rambling, disconnected account, or silence. I knew however she had been in the ward for some years.

"I met the King and Queen quite often." She asserted. "Ghandi had tea with me. My father was an Admiral you know."

None of this I believed. I thought she was dementing and confabulating, creating her own mind pictures divorced from reality. Once or twice she would pause however and slip in a line or two of the well-known poem –The Walrus and the Carpenter by Lewis Carroll. The significance of this initially escaped me. She kept trotting out, a few lines,

"O Oysters," said the Carpenter,
"You've had a pleasant run!
Shall we be trotting home again?'
But answer came there none--
And this was scarcely odd, because
They'd eaten every one."

I thought she was eccentric and demonstrating her erudition. In front of the examiners, I confidently stated she had dementia and quoted her distorted personal account of meetings with grandees. The senior examiner reacted derisorily stating,

"Oh. That is all true," and the rationale for my diagnosis was in ruins. "She was secretary to the Vice-Roy of India and has an illustrious back-ground." he added to my dismay.

Disconsolately, I stared at probable failure in the oral and the wrecking of aspirations to pass the last hurdle to medical qualification. Then her lines of verse came to mind and with a bravado I did not feel, said,

"There is a distorted thought process, sir,"

"Where and when?" he barked and clutching at a straw, I hesitantly offered,

"In the verse."

"Yes," he agreed, "Reiteration." and the penny finally dropped. In a flash I realised that she kept repeating the same lines of verse over and over again and did have a disordered thought process. Satisfied that the underlying mental disturbance had been correctly understood, the examiner turned the conversation to safer ground. I answered the rest of the questions and passed the viva. I had learned the need for caution in interpreting conversations with mentally-ill patients.

Baker's loaf

I had an ambivalent relationship with another patient, Bernie Cook, who had Parkinson's disease. He was a delight to have as a patient and was always bright and cheerful. This despite a condition that caused tremor in his hands and creeping stiffness and immobility of joints which was inexorably slowing him up. Until early retirement, he had been a baker and would arrive in the consulting room with a brown paper bag smelling deliciously of newly-made bread. He also made his own beer.

"A wee loaf for your good lady and something for you," he would announce as he left the consultation. Inside a parcel would be a monstrous, freshly baked loaf of bread with a crisp succulent crust and two bottles of his best brew.

His condition steadily worsened, despite the latest medications I prescribed for him. A small man, his posture declined and he was nearly bent double and shuffled along. He refused to have home visits, but every two weeks he would turn up with his brown parcel to the envy of my partners. His wife was much younger and had taken a job as a secretary in the local bank, when their income had dropped on his retirement.

She occasionally telephoned to request a change in his medication. I recognised she was carrying a heavy burden of care. Theirs, despite disparity in age, had been a long, loving marriage. Belatedly, she said sorrowfully that, he has become very aggressive and sometimes hides himself from when I return home. "He seems frightened of me. He has started to walk around with a bread knife in his hand." I promised to check him out carefully on his next visit. He appeared a few days later in his usual good spirits despite his clinical condition.

"For your wife," as he thrust the usual parcel upon me. "A new recipe, I think she will like it." I thanked him. Then in the middle of a full physical and psychological check, he conversationally said with conviction,

"She is poisoning me you know. Sally is putting poison in my bread!" I now was faced with the strange situation that Sally believed that he was out to knife her and he believed she was poisoning him! His mental examination did not reveal any other thought distortion, but this was a tricky home situation. Sally might well be attacked by her husband. He had developed paranoid delusions and was no longer always identifying her as his wife, but seeing her as an enemy.

I also wondered about his distorted thinking and the possibility that he might introduce poison into his bread, if he became disenchanted with me or confused about my role. His regular, generous gifts lost much appeal. I wondered whether the bread and contents should be analysed and nibbled round the crust rather than devouring the loaf as usual. With reservations, I could not resist quaffing his excellent beer. Sadly the presents would not continue for much longer however.

An early psychiatry referral was organised and his disturbed mental state confirmed by the consultant. Medication did little to help his organic brain disease and he deteriorated very quickly. Admitted to the long-stay dementia unit, he only lived a short time longer. I missed his cheery visits and his bread presentations and long recalled his baking skills when biting into a mundane super-market loaf.

Self diagnosis

Fred was another delightful, elderly gentleman who had worked all his life in a publishing house, before retiral. He was a voracious book reader and never travelled anywhere without the current book he was reading clutched in hand, His visits were rare, but we always had a chat about books for I enjoyed a good novel. He would present me with one he had particularly enjoyed and we would chat about the characters before the formal consultation began. For many years he had solicitously cared for a severely disabled wife. When she died his visits became more frequent and he grieved at her loss.

His behaviour began to change and receptionists' would retrieve his books from the surgery environs when he forgot to retrieve them. Always very courteous and correct with the staff Bette reported one day that he had been abusive to them. They had been taken aback at his out-burst of shouting. Always a smart dresser in suit, matching shirt and tie, his apparel became dishevelled. We wondered if his wife had previously supervised his dressing habit. He began to miss appointments, or turned up on the wrong day. I began to suspect that he was being overtaken by dementia and Julia the social worker reported. His home conditions are deteriorating, I do not think he can care for himself anymore.

Fred arrived very late one evening for a surgery appointment, obviously unaware of time and date. As he sat down opposite me, he burst in to a description of a book, but his discourse soon tailed off and he halted. Disconsolately he restarted, but words failed him, then haltingly,

"I think I am losing my mind Doctor."

"What makes you think that?" I queried.

"Because I ....I cannot remember." Then he fished a paper from his pocket and handed it to me. "I wrote this for you." I read the words slowly. He had written a poem – a potted personal case history. It read,

Confused

Just a line to say I'm living
that I'm not among the dead,
Though I'm getting more forgetful
and mixed up in my head.
I've got used to my arthritis
to my dentures I'm resigned,
I can manage my bifocals,
but, Oh, God, I miss my mind.
For sometimes I can't remember
when standing at foot of stair,

if, I must go up for something
or, have just come down from there?
And before the fridge so often,
My poor mind is filled with doubt.
Have I just put food away or,
have I come to take it out?
There are times in dark of night
when memory has a fight
I don't know if I am retiring,
or, putting on the light.
Of these events, I've got to write
I don't want to be a bore
Do try to put me right
but, have I written this before?
Am I dementing?
If so, I want to fight
Don't tell me if,
the answer, will fail to make me bright

I temporised in my response. He had written this with insight. "You are not alone, I forget things all the time" I empathised.

Sadly, when Fred took some formal Dementia Assessment tests, the score confirmed that he had Alzheimer's disease and his brain function was being destroyed by a dementing process. This was probably accelerated by the loss of his wife of 65 years. His decline was rapid.

I never did confirm his self-diagnosis with him. We both were aware of the prognosis and fortunately he did not live long aware of this affliction. His memory failed completely and he became unaware of time, place or state of well-being. He was admitted to the Poor Law Hospital and for a short time mindlessly wandered the wards, always clutching a book, which he could no longer appreciate. He deteriorated mentally and physically and was soon gone and so too my supply of novels. I missed our chats and when keys, wallet, papers were mislaid, a regular occurrence in my working day, I would remember his poem and wonder if dementia was also coming my way.

The Flying Scotsman

"How far did I fly Doc?" was Ben's opening question at the start of the consultation. My thoughts were jolted from the trivial routine of morning surgery and I jumped to the conclusion that he was referring to a recent vacation.

"You mean on holiday?" I responded guardedly.

"No. No! The day I flew off the mountain," he replied forcefully and I was reminded of a distant time when we were both members of the same climbing club and often walked together in the Grampian Mountains. I could not recall any mountain flights however.

Playing for time, I added,

"It's some time since we were out together."

"Ten or eleven years", he interjected, leaving me none the wiser. Apologetically, I added,

"My memory fails me for I cannot recall our last outing."

"Of course you do, you cannot possibly forget the occasion," he retorted angrily.

Taken aback by his vehemence, "I hastily raked back through my climbing memories, without further enlightenment. Loudly and aggressively he continued,

"It was the most remarkable thing to ever to happen to me."

"A lot has happened over these intervening years," I said defensively,

"You cannot have forgotten. It was the most momentous event I have ever experienced," and he pounded on the desk to emphasise his point. I apprehensively edged my seat further along the desk and away from him. To my dismay, he followed this manoeuvre by lunging further towards me.

Ben was a big, burly fellow in fair physical condition despite being in his sixties. He made an intimidating figure, becoming more so as his testiness turned to ire and anger. I wondered for the first time if a desk-mounted panic button might have had its place in the surgery.

I endeavoured to establish some rapport with him and asked,

"What hill were we on?"

"Ben Challum," he responded and I was no further forward, recalling no such location. Striving for elusive common communication, I tentatively ventured,

"Oh, a great day." His response was derisory.

"Great day! It was a disaster. I could have died instead of flown. You must remember, I was the first Flying Scotsman - Icarus personified."

Now I was really in trouble. For me the Flying Scotsman was the east coast train service from Edinburgh to London, aptly named after the lead locomotive "The Mallard" took the steam engine world speed record in 1938 with a speed of 125mph.I could not conceive a link between a mountain, train and Icarus. Study of the Classics had never been my strong point, but I was aware that Icarus had flown to disaster.. The connection eluded me as Ben lurched to his feet and lumbered round to my side of the desk.

Now towering above me, I edged beyond the confines of the desk gauging the distance to be covered between desk, exit door and safety. I temporised, humouring him with,

"Of course you flew. Quite remarkable. Nothing quite like it. The "Flying Scotsman." It must have been a record."

"How far did I fly?" he queried with increasing agitation. He was now jumping up and down, beside me. "I flew, I flew."

Seeking to pacify him, I agreed and suggested a flight path of several metres, "More than three or four metres," he ejaculated." Thirty metres and more. You must remember." He faced up to me with clenched fists. My retreat was cut off by a filing cabinet and it seemed physical attack was imminent. The desk telephone-link with reception was out of reach. I now believed that I was in the company of a schizophrenic, with very disturbed processes. How could I escape from this imbroglio?

Struggling for a solution, I remembered a recent course that I had attended. Neuro-linguistic programming was an innovative means of dealing with patients who had psychological problems. The techniques had been simplistic, but I had had no previous opportunity to practice them. One instruction suggested, was to mirror the gestures and behaviour of a disturbed patient, as this was often calming. They could be induced into then following the therapist's gestures.

I tentatively stepped forward towards Ben and lifted my hands to mirror his gestures, half expecting a wild swipe in retaliation. He retreated a little but continued to jump up and down wildly. Feeling foolish, I mimicked his steps, jumping up and down in unison with his movements. Remarkably, he retreated further as I advanced. His agitation decreased and the threatening behaviour turned abruptly into conventional soft-voiced discourse.

"I have come for my pills Doc. We have been on holiday and I have nearly run out." His conversation continued as if there had been no emotional outburst. He responded sensibly to further questioning, "I have been in Vancouver, the flight was long-delayed and I did not get much sleep. I have been feeling a bit dizzy and disorientated." He subjected himself to a physical examination and some simple psychological tests. None of which were abnormal and he made no further reference to flying off a mountain.

He appeared to be suffering from sleep-lack and jet-lag, but these events hardly accounted for his bizarre behaviour. I arranged a further appointment for him to visit with his wife and returned to waiting humdrum consultations. Between patients, there were a few moments to wonder about his strange conduct.

He returned a month later to advise me that all his hospital investigations had been normal, but he was always feeling fatigued and was struggling to manage at work. He made no further reference to flying even when prompted. Brain investigations were then rudimentary and did not go much beyond head x-ray and electro-encephalograph traces were often difficult to interpret.

Ben struggled on at work, often returning home after work to stay in bed until the time for work the next morning. Then one day, he called in to surgery very agitated. He had experienced a short episode when he had lost consciousness while watching television at home. Amy, his very worried wife, said the screen had showed flash-photographic scenes.

"He was twitching before and after the attack." This was a serious development for she was describing an epileptic seizure. What had been the trigger I wondered, as I arranged immediatc hospital referral.

After emergency admission, he suffered several full-blown convulsions in the ward. Finally a brain tumour was diagnosed after he lost power on one side of the body.He was operated upon. A meningioma tumour the size of a tennis ball was discovered and surgically removed. This was a benign lesion and despite its size he made a very good recovery.

"I am feeling fine," he announced six weeks later on a return visit to see me. "I need a final certificate stating I am fit for work please."

"How is the memory?" I asked.

"A bit patchy," Ben replied, "but it is much better than it was." then, "That was quite a day we last had together on the hills."

For a moment I feared a replay of his previous disturbing visit to the surgery, but he continued, "You really did save my life then. "

In the intervening weeks my own memory had finally recalled the walk we had done together, once from a remote glen over the high tops. Bad winter weather had delayed our departure for the mountains. Once en route, it had proved a long, hard day slogging over wet hills and difficult terrain. Darkness overtook us high up on a mountain ridge, with some miles to cover before reaching the safety of the car. We were tired. Both our head-torches had lost power and Ben's finally lost illumination. It was difficult to follow a compass-bearing on a trackless descent in the moonless night.

At one point Ben had forged ahead over a small bluff and as he disappeared from view, I suddenly realised that he was on the wrong route.

“Veer left,” I shouted to him.” Hearing my instruction, he turned sharply and abruptly disappeared from view. When I reached his position, the weak beam from my torch revealed we were on a cliff edge. There was a dark void in front of me and I shouted for Ben. There was a worrying silence, then to the left and quite a bit below came a response.

“I am down here.” Skirting the cliff edge I worked my way down the mountain, to ultimately find him perched on a narrow ledge, jutting out from the cliff-side. He was winded, but uninjured, except for bruising to a thigh and shoulder.

“I flew right off the mountain,” he announced. “If you had not called, I would have been right over that cliff and it seems to go down for ever,” as he peered to the right. The map confirmed several hundred metres of vertical cliff beside us. If he had gone over there, he would not have survived the fall. We took great care over the rest of the descent and parted on our separate ways.

Over time I had completely forgotten about the incident, until prompted by the strange vagaries of memory. Ben's brain lesion had distorted his recall of the incident and had fixed on the moment when he left terra firma. He did, for a few seconds, fly out into space. My memory of the event had been buried, until stimulated by the bizarre encounter with him in the office.

Happily his recovery was maintained, he returned to work. I saw him infrequently, but when we met he invariably stated that I had saved his life. A sixth-sense premonition that we were off-route and my timely shout had certainly saved him from serious mishap. Mischance and perchance often seemed to determine some of the mishaps which befell patients. In this encounter with Ben, underlying pathology with distortion of memory had triggered the event.

Strange Predicaments

It was a routine call after morning surgery to Mary Miller, a harassed young mother of four lively children who rarely made house call requests. She apologetically announced that none of the kids was seriously ill, but she would appreciate a visit for the youngest Christina, the six year old. An epidemic of minor intestinal infection was sweeping through the practice area. The call-list was long, but her house was on my visit-route and I said,

"I'll be in to see you shortly" and added her name to the list.

She was swabbing the kitchen floor when I arrived at her small house in a nearby village. Her usually trim and neat auburn hair was dishevelled and she looked more distraught than usual. She greeted me apologetically,

"I have been up all night with them and John has just been sick again, but they are getting better. They have all had sickness and diarrhoea and I couldn't bring them to the surgery. I was trying to keep them in bed and on fluids only, as you advised before." she explained. "It's difficult to keep them confined, but now Chris is complaining of ear pain and headache and is burning up."

I had a soft spot for Christina, who had spina bifida, a genetic spinal abnormality which made her incontinent and robbed her of mobility. She was courageous, always had a smile for me, never complained and tried desperately to share the active life of her brothers and sister who doted upon her.

This morning Mary had obviously lost the battle to restrain her unruly brood. Despite their affliction, the children were playing boisterously around the bed as Christina peered up at me anxiously from under a protective mound of blankets. She was surrounded by toys lovingly placed at her side by siblings.. Her cheeks were rose-red, she was sweating. I did not need the thermometer reading to confirm she had a high temperature. She obediently let me look in her ear where I could see a bulging red ear drum, which confirmed she had otitis media, an ear infection. Small children who become over-heated often have a convulsion and it was important to cool her down.

"Off with all the blankets," I said authoritatively, "you are stoking the furnace. We need to let her cool down. If you sponge her all over with tepid water and let it evaporate off a few times, it will bring her temperature down. I will give you some medicine to cure the infection." Penicillin was not always indicated for the condition, but she needed protection from further infection.

"I will give you some nice strawberry-tasting syrup to put you right." I reassured the little girl.

As I had a long list of further domiciliary visits, I was glad to make a speedy consultation, with an easy diagnosis and relevant treatment. With mum's help, the painful ear would soon improve and I hastened to complete my call round. I scribbled a prescription, bid the little girl farewell, navigated round the many playthings adorning the floor and prepared to leave. Mary escorted me to the door and as I stepped outside, I thought I heard a plaintive cry.

"Help me, help me," in a wavering almost inaudible cry. I checked my step.

"Was that Christina?" I queried, but Mary had heard nothing from within the house. I hesitated, but there was silence and I made my way back to the car, until again,

"Help me. Help somebody." The words were very faint and almost out of ear-shot. I looked around but saw no one in the neighbouring line of detached bungalows. I peered up the road - empty but for my parked car - then strode back up the drive and stopped to listen again. Silence reigned despite a wait of several minutes. The local residents were all at work. Reassured that it was probably children at play, I turned to be on my way, as there was nothing untoward in sight.

Then again, distant wavering cries of "Help. Help." from somewhere round the back of the properties. I recommenced the vigil, this time looking further afield along neat back gardens. Peripheral, ubiquitous, colour-coded local authority rubbish bins stood in serried mini-ranks, behind each house. An unremarkable scene, my search turned to the rear of houses in the next street, where activity finally caught my eye. Two feet were waving out of a distant bin! The next cry centred from there. I hurried behind several houses to reach one owned by one of my elderly lady patients. She was a former teacher and a tiny little sparrow of a woman in her late eighties. She lived on her own and was always known respectfully as Miss Devine.

Rounding the corner of the house, I saw two giant wheeled-bins lying on their side and an upright third containing Miss Devine, who was vertically inverted and face down in the bin. It took mere moments to extricate her by pulling the bin onto its side and hauling her out. Her skirts had fallen over body and head and were stifling her. She was breathless, swollen and blue of face and had a misshapen shoulder.

"What happened?" I demanded as I lifted her bodily and took her into the bungalow." She struggled to speak,

"I was putting the rubbish out .....and.... and...as I leaned over the bin,... my specs. fell off....... I had to stand on the side of the other bin to get at them..... and as I leaned over... it went from under my feet and I pitched in." she puffed and wheezed. "I banged my arm and landed on my head and came over all funny..... My clothes were smothering me. I couldn't get out.....No one seemed to hear me. I thought I was going to die."

I wondered how long she would have survived in this relatively deserted neighbourhood if I had not fortuitously heard her calls of distress. She was very small - less than five feet tall - and so light, I felt I was carrying a child as I eased her on to the bed. Clinical examination revealed some fluid in her lungs and dislocation of a shoulder. I organised an ambulance to take her to emergency care. She recovered well and thereafter always referred to me as her guardian angel. I never failed to be amazed at the predicaments people could get themselves in.

Up the Ladder

I recalled another occasion when driving along a street on another house call. I saw Jack Fellows, a patient of mine, painting the highest point of wood-work under the eaves on the front of his house. He was perched five metres high up a ladder, which was resting on a trestle located on a path above a sunken garden. A large can of paint was in one hand, as he stretched out with the paint brush in the other hand to reach the apex of the house. I prepared to give him a passing hand-wave, idly thinking this was a rather foolhardy procedure and hoped the paint tin was not full in the event of mishap. No sooner the thought than the inevitable occurred!

"Off you go." came from up the ladder. His female partner, who had been steadying the trestle, moved aside. As she turned to depart, she left the contraption unsupported and out of equilibrium. Stepping away, the trestle canted and as in a slow motion, lap-stick comedy film, tragedy unfolded. As the support fell over, the ladder began to slide sideways down the wall. The painter, still with brush-arm extended, commenced a rapid descent down the side of the wall. As the ladder gained momentum, the trestle was pushed away from the wall towards the sunken garden a metre below.

"Look out, I am going," shouted the painter belatedly.

A squeal of anguish came from Julia his wife. As she looked upwards, trestle and descending ladder fell upon her, bearing her bodily off the path and into the garden below. Her husband inexorably continued his unexpected flight downwards, leaving a long trail of brushed white paint to mark his descent down the house. The paint-tin then flew out of his hand and the contents poured liberally over the scene below, with some sailing over my car, to land on the other side of the street. Trestle, ladder and painter finally landed on top of the woman and the last of the paint bespattered the garden, as the tin completed its fall.

There was no further sound from the victim under the debris, I braked to a halt, grabbed my emergency bag and rushed to give assistance. Splashing through a widening pool of white paint, I grabbed the ladder, which was lying aslant the destroyed legs of the trestle and moved it aside. Jack struggled to his feet. He lifted a twisted hand towards me, the fingers clenched, but for two at right angles to each other, which were obviously broken. Remarkably, he had survived the fall otherwise physically unscathed. I turned my attention to the woman.

Julia was a house-proud young woman who dressed in fashion. On my professional visits, her fastidious ways were reflected in house contents designed to perfection. She took pride in her appearance which was always immaculate, with clothing elegant and stylish. Her apparel had now become of minor consideration.

Under the downward onslaught of ladder, trestle, partner and paint, she had not fared well. She was lying under the remains of the trestle, liberally covered with paint, now reddening with blood from a facial wound. I wondered if she had survived the catastrophe. As I pulled off distorted angle-irons from over her, it appeared she had been knocked-out by a blow from the steelwork. The falling trestle had thrust her body a metre down on to stone slabs in the sunken garden, before ladder and falling Jack reached their final resting places on top of her. As she lay injured, she suffered the final ignominy of a liberal bespattering from a cascade of descending paint. Face, hair and upper body were covered with still-flowing paint, now dripping on to the ground.

Clinical examination was difficult.

"What have I done to you lass?" her anguished husband wailed as he pulled off the steel wreckage,

"Don't move her," I ordered, concerned that she might have a broken back, or neck, in the accident. I was too late; he lifted her from the garden and laid her on the path before I could intervene. A passer-by joined us and offered handkerchiefs to tackle the paint, so that I could identify the site of the wound. As I cleared away blood and paint she stirred.

"What happened?" she groaned.

"You have had an accident, but you are fine," I assured her although uncertain of the extent of her injuries."

"It was my fault." the conscience-stricken husband burst in as he held her hand.

"You told me to go off shopping," she whispered hesitantly,

"Yes, I thought it was all secure, and it happened in a second" he asserted.

Relieved that she was now conscious, I checked that she was pain-free. Shocked, she had no obvious injuries, other than a laceration to her face, to which I applied adhesive sutures. These immediately peeled off again, failing to adhere on skin that was far from paint free.

"What is your name," as I tested her mental status. She could not remember her name or intimate details, was suffering from concussion and needed hospital attention. I rang the emergency unit to advise the casualty doctor of her impending arrival and need for treatment.

"It's a paint job and concussion." I advised. "A paint job?" He questioned, "Yes, you will need a lot of paint remover." He did not take my words literally and quipped. "Is it not a paint shop you need," as he rang off, which ensured nurses were unprepared for her admission.

As I journeyed to the nearby hospital in the ambulance with them both, Jack explained that he believed ladder and trestle were securely tied to a down pipe on the house wall, until moving them to the other side of the door. There, in the absence of a light-fitting support, he had called Julie, (about to depart on a shopping trip), to steady his precarious stance. She unwillingly agreed to help. In his anxiety to free her for her shopping, he had misjudged the stability of his stance. He waved her off prematurely, initiating the string of events leading to disaster.

On her arrival, hospital staff used all the store of paint-removing fluid in the hospital, just to remove paint from her face. By this time it had hardened. For weeks thereafter she and family members combed paint from her hair. Fortunately she suffered no serious permanent damage from the incident other than a small scar from the laceration. Both had been very lucky to survive a fall which could have killed or permanently disabled them. Jason, the local window cleaner, also a patient, perched just a few rungs up his ladder had fallen off a few weeks previously. A minor fall compared to this incident, he was paralysed below the waist thereafter and his window cleaning days were over.

The partnership survived this threat to her well being. She did not blame Jack for the injury, but was furious at the damage done to her best coat and skirt. She was left however, with one other memento of the accident. She developed a phobia for ladders and wisely refused to assist him in further DIY house tasks.

Road Accident

I spent much time driving to house calls and inevitably came upon road accidents. They always reminded me of my first day in the practice, but fortunately few were as serious. On one occasion a car shot across the T junction in front of me and ploughed into the gate pillars of a nearby house drive. As I watched, a ripple ran along the abutting wall, which collapsed on to the pavement. The bonnet of my own car had nearly been struck as the other passed ahead. With some choler, I exited my vehicle to accost the other driver. Anger dissipated as I approached, for the car was still in automatic gear and was striving mightily to complete the destruction of the pillar. The driver an elderly man was

A FATHER'S EXPERIENCE

Parenting Teens

- OWUSU ANSA BOAFO -

still inside and unconscious.

As I hurried to his aid, the house occupant rushed forward. An off-duty fire-fighter, he was accustomed to retrieving victims strapped in cars. As I opened the nearside door the opposite one was opened and a face peered in. I recognised the local clergyman who lived across the road. The driver was being succoured by doctor, fireman and priest within seconds of the incident. He seemed well prepared for a potential terminal life event!

It proved a difficult task to extricate the comatose man, as his foot had become jammed over the accelerator pedal, keeping the engine on full power to continue its encounter with the gate-post. It lost the battle and also collapsed. The car surged forward to be halted by the stone debris. John, the fireman, went off to fetch a crow-bar to free the foot.

"Last rites," the priest questioned, but I had found the carotid pulse and the patient was still alive. John returned and the lever was applied, the imprisoned appendage prised free and the engine power neutralised. The patient was laid on the roadside and an ambulance soon sped off with him to hospital. He had suffered a cerebral thrombosis - a blood clot in the brain - but recovered completely. The police arrived to survey a scene of minor devastation. Thirty metres of fallen masonry testified to the force of an impact which, but for the grace of a few seconds, had nearly struck me. I rather shakily continued on my way brooding about serendipity, good fortune and laws of chance.

An Untimely Demise

Sandy was a solidly built, rugged ex-commando, he rarely visited surgery, but I met him occasionally when his children were ill. He was modest and rarely could be encouraged to talk of his military past. Occasional hints that he had been involved in nefarious global activities and special training suggested that he had once been in the SAS. A countryside ranger, he worked enthusiastically in youth work for the local community and had a solid reputation as a reliable leader and instructor. He was keen on outdoor pursuits and I would occasionally meet him in the high mountains where he often bivouacked, irrespective of inclement weather. Mountaineering, raft-running on river rapids and canoe marathons saw him braving the elements, imperturbable and unfazed by trauma and drama. On occasion, we teamed up, I found him to be tough, resilient and resourceful, when facing the occasional risky events that come with adventure sports. Medically, he was a model of good health. A non-smoker of lean proportions, muscular and brawny, he shrugged off bouts of influenza that felled his pals. The picture of robust well-being, his outdoor life encouraged fitness. He categorised the ideal GP. practice patient, one who attracted an annual Government funded fee as a patient, but never used health services.

The wife was the converse of her husband. She abhorred the great outdoors and her adventures embraced only shopping expeditions. I wondered what other attributes had drawn them together. Photographs revealed he had been a fine looking soldier in his dress uniform. Medals attested to courage and expertise. They had married late producing a gentle, rather feckless, unassuming boy and a sprightly girl. The son was not built like the father and had the personality of Mum, a squeeky-speaking little lady. Jane the daughter embarked upon a nursing career. I would meet her occasionally when she took up a post in the district general hospital.

Wife Judy became a regular visitor with minor complaints. As often the case, she presented with physical symptoms when the underlying problem was a psychosocial one. Family doctors were given scant psychological and psychiatric training in the fifties as undergraduates and none thereafter. Most GPs. had little regard for complaints relating to the psyche, at a time when there was little effective treatment for depression and major psychiatric illness. Electro-convulsive therapy was the resource of last resort.The repulsive application of electric current to the skull seemed a barbaric, mediaeval form of torture to most medical practitioners.

Gradually, over much time listening to trivial health complaints presented in a doleful voice, I won her confidence and she admitted to having a clandestine affair with another man. A God-fearing and strict Methodist and a zealous attender at church on the Sabbath, she was mentally engaged in a fight with conscience, church dogma and her betrayal of Sandy. The inner mental conflict was surfacing as physical symptoms for which she felt justified in seeking medical aid. Her anxiety and mental impasse brought insomnia, migraines and irritable bowel symptoms. She became a very frequent surgery attender. Separation of a married couple was rare in these days. Divorce was legally difficult and stigma attached to divorcees. As she could not change her situation without giving up her new relationship, she became another “heart sink patient”. I could do little to help and dreaded her frequent visits. The regular consultations became a prop for her, as she continued the illicit liaison of which her husband remained unaware.

“Sandy is a good man and husband, but he is never at home she would comment. She would not consider any suggestion that she discuss her quandary with her husband and consider leaving him. Her Victorian upbringing and religious scruples would not contemplate deserting the man she had married. I became resigned to her continued regular attendances, which always over-ran the allotted appointment time. She had a whinging voice and always left me feeling I had failed as a doctor to improve her wellbeing. She needed the help of a psychologist. None was available in the local NHS and she refused to accept that the root cause of her symptoms was mental conflict; I could only treat the symptoms and not the cause.

Although Sandy rarely appeared for consultation, I stumbled on one of his mountain hideaways when out walking in rugged climbing country. His climbing companion, with whom he was sharing a tent, was a rather mannish female lawyer. Mixed-sex camping was rare then even within the camaraderie of mountaineering and it was not apparent whether this was a paramour or a climbing buddy. ”Gay” was then associated with “jolly, happy and bright”, had no other connotations. I did not choose to explore the intricacies of this relationship. It did seem however that his wife might have found a way out of her dilemma, if she had been aware of his new partnership. Both however continued apparently unaware that each was intriguing against the other. I was sorely tempted to reveal the situation, but was ethically bound to confidentiality. The impasse seemed set to continue. I suffered many more time-consuming consultations before events took an unexpected turn when she arrived particularly agitated in surgery, one morning.

“Sandy hasn’t returned home,” she complained. I was unsure whether this was a relief for her, or a penance. He had apparently left the previous morning on a practice run for an impending mountaineering/cycling/boating marathon and had not been seen since. After a two night absence, the police had been informed, but had been unable to trace him. The couple had had a marital tiff before his departure and he had left without revealing his route. Doubly guilt-stricken by her misconduct and their parting in enmity, she suffered anguish for several days, unsure whether he had discovered her disloyalty and had left her, or had come to harm in some wild place.

A telephone call came from Bette in the surgery office.

"Call into the mortuary on your rounds. They have a case for you. They have not given any name," she advised.

As local police doctor, I was often called to police investigations and an unidentified body apparently awaited for examination in the post mortem room at the district hospital. There were no details and no urgency was suggested. I procrastinated until after surgery work was over before making the post-mortem visit.

The normal mortuary porter was ill. Out of conventional working hours, a staff nurse was temporarily responsible in his place. On this occasion the stand-in was Sandy's daughter, Jane was now a fully trained nurse. I had come to know her professionally. She had become a staff nurse in the geriatric unit. I also worked there as a hospital practitioner caring for four wards of geriatric patient in an old Poor Law Hospital. She had been on duty one morning when an embarrassing event occurred.

It was the custom for the nursing staff to defer the completion of a death certificate, which was my responsibility, until the morning, if an anticipated death occurred during the night in a patient known to be terminally ill. This practice saved me from many night interruptions for a hospital visit to sign a piece of paper. Conventionally, the cadaver was prepared for burial, placed in a shroud and barrowed to the mortuary to await my morning visit.

As I entered the ward on this occasion Jane announced,

"Mr. Johnson died at 2am. He is in the mortuary," and I set off to make the post mortem examination. The mortuary was in an out-house. A bare sterile place, it held six refrigerated drawers in a bank on one wall. The only furniture was a wheeled single deck patient transport trolley draped with a sheet, which overhung almost to the floor.. This stood just inside the door. From long established habit the long-serving porter would leave my patient on the trolley, so that I could make a quick examination before the transfer to the cold store.

I bounded into the mortuary and advanced on the trolley, to note that it was empty. Assuming the body was in a drawer, I worked my way along the bank but all were empty. Back again in the ward, I accosted Jane,

"Where is Mr. Johnson?" When wards were very busy, sometimes the dead patient was left in a side room.

"In the mortuary, she replied."

"No. He is not there."

"The porter took him down before he went off duty" she assured me.

"Have another look." Grudgingly I returned to the mortuary, confirmed the body was neither on the trolley, or in any of the drawers and rather crossly returned to the ward. "It's not there. Where is it? The porter has gone off duty," said sister intervening. "He is a 'temp' as Andie is off sick. The patient must be in a side-room."

A search of ward and side-rooms was however to no avail and sister, Jane and I revisited the mortuary without finding the body. In panic mode a further search was made and unsuccessful efforts made to contact the porter. On the chance that the undertaker had removed the body prematurely, he was contacted, but denied any intervention. The event was now taking on serious overtones. Had the body been snatched? Memories of Burke and Hare's historic grave-robbing came to mind. Matron informed me that the Hospital Board and police must be informed and I temporised. I could see in my mind's eye, the headlines in the next issue of the Harborough Herald. "Local Doc loses body!"

Stalling her intent for a few minutes, I made one more despairing visit to the morgue and once again peered into six empty drawers. Reluctantly I had to accept we had lost the body! As I forlornly opened the exit door, the empty trolley attracted my eye. I absent-mindedly straightened the draped sheet over the top of the trolley which was slightly askew. It slid aside a few inches and there was a momentary glimpse of underlying sheeting. I whipped off the drape and there lay the enshrouded Mr. Johnson. There was unusually a second shelf on this trolley. Mightily relieved, I certified his death and avoided a scandal. The combination of a new porter and a replacement two tiered trolley and the placing of the corpse on the second shelf had misled us all.

Sadly, the unwanted attention brought to this procedure ended the cosy arrangement I had with night-time deaths. For some time thereafter, until memories dimmed, I had to travel to the hospital to certify a death before the staff duty change. Jane used to occasionally remind me of this affair when we met professionally on the wards.

She was always affable and now greeted me with a few pleasantries adding as a tease.

"Not lost any more bodies doctor?" "One is enough." I retorted as we went to the hospital's cold storage room, where a bank of large refrigerated drawer trays held cadavers awaiting identification and burial.

She strolled over to the bank and identified an unnamed label. A routine task, she nonchalantly pulled out the drawer, whipped back the shroud, stood mesmerised for a long moment, paled and collapsed in shock to the floor. I stepped forward to discover that her father, was lying inert and waxen-faced within. The corpse had been identified with profound familial psychic impact.

Sandy had been found dead in the country-side. Following standard police practice, when there was no identification on the person and the victim unknown, the body was transported to the mortuary, so that further enquiry might be made as to identity. Cause of death was not immediately apparent but, there was no evidence of physical injury. The police did not question the solidity of the twenty year marriage and did not suspect foul play. Further pathological investigation revealed that Sandy had a genetic heart anomaly of which he and the military had been unaware. He could have died at any time since childhood.

Paradoxically, I saw very little of Judy after this sudden loss of spouse. Bereavement counselling was apparently provided by the clandestine partner who divorced shortly after. The once illicit relationship flourished and led ultimately to remarriage. Her trivial medical complaints disappeared and if she had feelings of guilt, they were buried with her husband.

Jane could have been permanently psychologically traumatised by this unfortunate tragedy, but she displayed some of the toughness of her father's personality. Aided by her professional training and the resilience of youth, she shortly afterwards met an admirer, married and emigrated.

The small, wispy and ineffectual son drifted in and out of jobs and marriages. Unlike his tough, resilient and robust father he was psychologically fragile. He began to present at surgery with minor complaints generated by mental rather than physical causes. In time, he admitted to feelings of inferiority and awareness that he had never met his father's expectations, but missed him sorely. He became a drifter drawing state financial benefits. I had replaced one "heart sink" patient with another.

The cycle was being repeated, I wondered if the relationship would again be ended in an untimely, sudden death. He ultimately met a girl with similar tendencies, paired up and went off with her to end my professional relationship. Many years later, I heard that after a protracted and disastrous spell cohabiting with this girl, she had spent his savings and left him for another. In despair he had taken an over-dose of drugs and died. I wondered whether this unfortunate saga might have ended differently if his father had remained on the scene.

Serendipity

There were a few occasions in my career when chance played a significant part in saving lives. Over time I came to know patients, families and addresses well. On the house-visit round, I collected house-call requests from surgery staff, neighbours and telephone contacts. I did not always write them down, relying on memory to guide me to the correct rendezvous. This system occasionally failed me. I would turn up to a house similar in appearance to my intended destination, but in the wrong street.

One day I breezed into a house in a small housing estate with identical houses in similarly designed streets and almost collided with an older woman - the family grandmother - a patient of mine, who was rushing out. Mrs. Johnson greeted me

"Thank goodness you are here. Maisie's just choked. In here!"

I entered the living room to see a four year old girl clutched in the lap of a terrified young mum. She was trying to fish food from the little one's mouth with a finger. The child's face was blue-black with cyanosis from lack of oxygen. She was gasping convulsively, desperately striving for air through a blocked airway. She had choked and was dying before our eyes.

The Heimlich procedure is the recommended means of relieving this kind of food obstruction. I grabbed the wee girl from Mum.

"Quick. Give her to me," I commanded and gripped Maisie with my arms folded round her upper abdomen. Giving a sudden powerful thrust into the belly,I up-ended her. A bolus of food shot from her mouth. Frenzied breathing attempts sucked in air. Her facial colour immediately flushed and she began to cry, to be consoled by a very relieved mother. The emergency was over and grandmother spoke,

"My Doctor, that was marvellous, we thought we were going to lose her. She was just eating her breakfast when she choked. We didn't know what to do and she was going blue and could not breathe. I was rushing next door for the telephone to ring the surgery when you appeared. It was miraculous."

Choking over a food obstruction which blocks the airway can kill adults. Children are particularly vulnerable and less able to withstand such an event. Emergency intervention has to be immediate and the first aid manoeuvre carried out within seconds to guarantee air flow and survival. Within four minutes of obstruction, there can be irreversible brain damage and death. On checking my call-list I discovered that I had gone to a different street and house than the one requested address in the book. Chance had intervened, Maisie was lucky and my wrongly-directed house call had saved her life.

These fortuitous interventions occurred intermittently over the years, especially with patients who were on the regular routine visit list and received a house visit monthly, usually on set days. I would be driving in the neighbourhood with no thought for a particular patient at all and one not on the call list. Out of the blue, a niggling concern about them would creep into my thoughts, which I would endeavour to resist. It would become more dominant and demanding. I would reluctantly make an unscheduled visit, to often find the patient in urgent need of medical intervention. Serendipity, or thought transference? Whichever, these fortunate forebodings were difficult to ignore. Unscheduled visits often brought happy outcomes

The Artisans

"I'll dae ye in." Tony threatened aggressively. He was an objectionable, truculent "druggie". Unkempt, uncouth and foul of language, I had just refused to give him controlled drugs to feed his addiction. It was another very busy Monday morning of surgery consultations after a long weekend on call duty. Several, night-time visits had forced me unwillingly from bed and sleep had been badly disrupted. There was a long list of house visits awaiting the end of office consultations and it was a grey and dismal day outside. I had gradually come to dread a Monday morning after the weekend on call and this particular one had not started well.

"Feel free." I countered Tony's threat, contemplating in my current state of mind that death might be a welcome release from the daily grind. I regarded him disdainfully. He had only part-use of one arm which was palsied and the fingers in the other hand were clawed. Personal onslaught on his veins with infected needles had paid a heavy price in disability. Nevertheless he still injected drugs where he could. He had one redeeming feature - an artistic bent. He could cut wonderful head profiles of people from wadded sheets of paper. Despite his infirmities, he could still reproduce a silhouetted likeness of a head in a few minutes. I had once marvelled at his skill when he had produced one of me. Thereafter he often tried to cajole me into giving him a desired drug prescription by making further caricatures. I resisted his blandishments however.

"Get out," I ordered, as I called his bluff and escorted him off the premises. He would be back to try his luck again in a few days, with another pack of lies to wheedle drugs from a resistant partner. Tired and apathetic, I gloomily wondered about a doctor's lot and the wisdom of practising a profession exposed to such onerous public demands. GPs. were contracted to a 24 hour per day, 365 day per year service commitment to attend to patients. Partners retained a personal list of patients and conjoined lists could include 18-20,000 patients. This ensured a large clinical demand upon the on-call doctor out of traditional consulting hours. Revisits also had to be fitted in around conventional consultations. They were a tedious, tiring burden for the doctor who had worked the weekend, before he could go off duty on Monday evening.

Consultations were booked at five minute intervals. We relied on "quickies" involving only the issue of a simple prescription, or "unfit to work "certificate to speed patients through the two hour consulting session. Inevitably surgeries over-ran. It only needed one difficult diagnosis, or in-depth interview, for the besieged doctor to run far over the allotted time, delaying even further, awaiting house calls consultations.

The Miner

Many sick patients came for consultation, and deserved every moment of their allotted time. The chronic cardiac and bronchitic patients presented with swollen ankles, chest pain and breathlessness and little could be offered them in medications. The armamentarium of curative drugs was tiny. I could at best alleviate and rarely cure. Patients rarely complained about their disability and many kept going at work against my wishes. Tom Collier was one of these. He came from a long line of miners and would not consider working above ground, despite severe bronchitis.

My amateur home-based DIY and construction efforts made me aware of inadequacies in industrial health and safety care. This had affected many of my patients in their work place. Health and Safety Regulations were weak and work-practices unchanged since Victorian times. Polluted air, smoke-ridden rooms and dangerous work environments were commonplace. They lead to many avoidable accidents and much chronic illness. The majority of adults also smoked cigarettes at a time when the cancerous effects were unappreciated.

There were many miners on the practice list of which Tom Collier was one. He belonged to a team of hard-working men working in a local colliery. They set off for their underground shift early in the morning and would return in the evening. They plodded back through the town with blackened, faces, hands and clothes. Most still lived in miner's houses where the wife would be waiting for the return, with a tin-bath full of steaming water placed in front of the earth. Pit-head baths were a luxury of the future.

When we first met in my early weeks in the practice, Tom was dressed in a well worn suit and was at first sight an office worker, until observing his calloused, black-streaked hands. I asked,

"Where do you work?" and was slightly surprised to be told,

"A' the coalege" I thought that he worked at the local technical college. In the following weeks, I was impressed by the number of the town's sturdy, tough young men who all seemed to be studying in further education. Then I realised that they were coal-miners working at the coal-edge and were in the elite band working at the coal-face.

Pit accidents were common and miners would present with terrible gashes in limbs and on hands which carried scars from past trauma. Tom had lost a family members in pit accidents and he had blue-black-scored wrists, arms and chest from ingrained coal-dust. They told the story of past mishaps. Like his fellows he had symptoms of chronic bronchitis and silicosis and a progressive shortage of breath, from work deep in the earth. Pneumoconiosis (black lung) deprived many of the ability to work. For a short time they laboured on the surface and then they were paid-off employment to linger with increasing dyspnoea and recurrent infection until premature death.

Tom became a regular surgery visitor as breathlessness robbed him of his vigour. His pale face, which rarely saw the sun, became blue-tinged as the blood lost its oxygenation. He resisted my suggestions that he should give up work and manfully turned up for his shift despite my misgivings. Politicians aware of the increasing cost of sickness benefit payments, sought to curtail them.They attempted to identify perceived malingerers who, fit to work, were on benefit and defrauding state funds. Miners, for ill- considered reasons, became targets for public scrutiny.

Tom became so incapacitated with chronic bronchitis and emphysema that he was unfit for any further work. His permanent incapacity was questioned however by bureaucrats, despite my explicit supportive testimony. He had become a 'blue bloater' in appearance, with swollen legs and blue-tinged skin the result of anoxia. He was housebound in his little miner's cottage, known as a 'but and ben,' which comprised two rooms with a lavatory in the minute back garden.

He remained uncomplaining on my visits despite continuing deterioration in his condition. To my,

"How are you today? "he always responded,

"So, so doctor, no' as bad as mony." He now needed to breathe supplementary oxygen to oxygenate his tissues. A four-foot high, black, gas cylinder stood on wheels by his bedside, testimony to his incapacity and a vital part of his treatment. The Benefits Agency insisted on additional justification of his invalid state and questioned that his work was a causative agency in his ill health, I unwillingly quizzed him about his work history and time at the coalface.

"How do you spend your day?" I asked, trying to discover how disabled he was. His answer puzzled me.

"Oh, I whittle away" he said. I thought he meant time passed slowly in his day, but he added. "There is always a new piece to carve. I'll show you what I do." As he pulled open a cupboard. It was full of wonderfully carved miniature animals, cars and buildings, all shaped in minute detail from coal fragment. Tom did not just hew coal, he fashioned it into small works of art. He was a very able sculptor but was modest about his craftsmanship.

"This keeps me busy and I sell some pieces." I commended him on his skill. Then thinking about this unlikely product extricated from his underground labours added.

"What is it like working down the pit?"

"It's a job. Ma faither done it as weel, Ma gran'faither was killed in a pithead accident. His wife had to bring up two weans on the money from a whip-round by his mates, after he died. There wis nae state benefits then," he spluttered between wheezes. Then, after a spasm of coughing, "if the Benefits folk knew the conditions we work in, none of them would grudge us our pensions." It occurred to me that I could not visualise working deep in the bowels of the earth and gave up on further inquisition.

"Ye should gae and see for yersel," he puffed as I left. His words stayed in mind.

Some of my forebears had worked and died in the collieries. With many miners on our list, perhaps I should have been more aware of their working environment. By chance the local mine manager appeared in surgery the next day for treatment for arthritis - a common condition in men who spent many hours in damp, wet surroundings..

Joe McColey was tall, burly and taciturn. He had a stoop from long working in a confined space. He had been a miner since becoming a pithead-errand boy at fourteen years age. A self-made man he had worked in all the mining jobs, educated himself through night-school after long work shifts, he was held in respect by employees.

Not known for wordy speech, he tended to give peremptory orders and rarely embroidered any conversation. Ascertaining his clinical problems often brought monosyllabic answers. As I examined his knee I conversationally mentioned,

"I was wondering about a visit to a pit." He grunted. "I was thinking it a good idea to see where many of my patients work." Another grunt and silence. Assuming the suggestion had not been welcome, I concentrated on the clinical problem, offered a prescription and he was on his way. To my surprise a telephone call came next day.

"Mr. McColey's secretary here. If you would care to come to the office on your next half day, you can go down the pit." Hoist again with my own petard, I slightly apprehensively turned up at the pit a few days later. McColey welcomed me dourly and passed me on to a grinning foreman,

"Takin' yer life in yer haunds," he joked. "Pit these oan," and he thrust overalls, a helmet and head torch at me. "Jist follow me and dae as a dae" as in moments he lumbered off.

Suitably attired, I followed even more concerned about personal safety. I wondered at the transient insane desire that had encouraged me to go below the the earth's surface. The new clothing seemed to make the man however. Looking the part, I adjusted rapidly to my new role, as I strode after him across the busy yard. The great, spoked wheels of the winding gear dominated the scene and conveyor belts were drawing coal newly-mined from the depths to be sorted. Bogies full of waste were being hauled air-borne to decant over bings and slag heaps leaked slurry into fearsome jet-black lagoons. Rail wagons full of black gold were being shunted by the pit rail pug. Buildings were overlain and ingrained with black dust. It was a noisy, dirty, miserable and dangerous environment, I was still on the surface, in daylight, in the rain on a bleak November day.

Hastily following Bob my mentor, I grabbed a tally from the overseer and followed him in to the cage for the lift descent into the ground. The gate was clanged shut, a bell rang. My stomach dropped as with dramatic suddenness we plunged into the dark. An unwelcome thought came to mind that my grandfather had been killed in a pit-shaft accident. The descent was death defying and prolonged. At last however we jerked to a halt at the base of the shaft in a narrow dimly-lit cavern jammed with moving conveyor belts and bogies. The walls were streaming with water and it seemed to gush in and out of narrow tunnels which pierced the Stygian gloom. Every move seemed fraught with danger.

Bob jumped into an empty bogie, I followed him in the next one on the conveyor belt. We plunged into a hell of narrow-walled, iron and wood-propped passage-ways running ever deeper into the ground. Steel girders stuck out from walls and electric light bulbs trailed from wires at rare intervals to relieve the engulfing gloom. Water dripped off walls and ceiling and surged intermittently from mini, wayside waterfalls.

We were careering through a man made Hades. I wondered fearfully about the omnipresence of 'deadly damps' I had heard Tom and his fellows talking about in the pub. They had tales of 'fatal black, fire, stink and white damp'.They were lethal mixtures of carbon dioxide, carbon monoxide and nitrogen which lurked about underground and could stealthily and explosively overcome the unwary miner.

At last this bucketing roller coaster was over and a linesman brought our crude steeds to a halt. Bob swung his feet over the side and was off down a narrow gallery. I perforce had to follow, now increasingly conscious of how far it was back to the shaft and the surface. The gallery was a bogie wide. We squeezed into one-man refuges as rail-bound tubs, over-loaded with huge coal chunks squealed and swayed past. The only light now was that from the head torch, with its narrow gleam showing the way ahead and failing to light the many hazards nearby.

The increasing noise of machinery heralded a coal-cutter at work and dust and pollution gusted back to envelop us. I marvelled for a few moments at the massive monster devouring the coalface, feeding coal back to subservient miners at a remarkable pace. As the shearer with its rotating cutters chewed into the fuel deposit, they laboured mightily to keep up with the voracious beast. They shovelled the coal it had digested into tubs to be hauled back to the surface.

We only stopped for a few moments however, then were off into an even narrower gallery with the ceiling dropping ever lower until it frequently bumped my helmet. After ten minutes of scrambling in ever more difficult conditions, a few lights heralded arrival at the coalface. A space the size of a large house room was supported by pillars of coal holding up the roof. In this restricted area, three miners were hewing a coal-seam about one metre thick. One was lying on his side wielding a pick-axe into the coal. The other cleared the fall and his mate sped it on its way to the far distant surface. This was where Tom had worked. For years he had risked life and limb a mile below the earth's surface in hellish conditions about a mile from the pithead, I marvelled at his endurance and survival.

Tom did not draw pension benefits for long after my underground venture. He deteriorated rapidly, could not care for himself and was admitted to the local miner's care home to re-join his work-mates. Surrounded by breathless, puffing, gasping ex-miners choking away their last days on earth, his days were numbered, So too were the many small pits in the area which were mercifully closed in ensuing years. Their redundant work force was recruited reluctantly into the embryonic information technology age.

The Artist

I was running very late dealing with a long consultation list and was not in a receptive frame of mind when the next patient entered. I did not know her and she demurely sat down and waited patiently without speaking. I searched for her record. It was out of place in my pile, adding to my frustration.

"What can I do for you?" I barked. She blanched and recoiled in the chair and I regretted the out-burst. This was not the way to embark on a fruitful doctor/ patient relationship.

"How are you keeping" I added in a conciliatory tone. There was no immediate response and the silence lengthened. Feeling guilty at starting off on the wrong foot, I did not seek to antagonise her further and remained quiet. Finally under the pressure of time, I interjected quietly,

"How can I help?" Tears flooded down her cheeks as she sobbed. Abandoning any hope of a quick consultation, I belatedly and compassionately tried to help. Her notes recorded a long history of physical illness, family tragedy, withdrawal from work and failed therapeutic intervention. When the sobbing abated, I finally was able to abstract her story and elicit an underlying untreated depression. Miss Whyte was at the end of her tether, her physical well-being and thinking processes worn down by life events. She lived alone, had little family support, was clinically depressed and possibly suicidal. She needed urgent attention but there were limitations on what I might provide.

Patients had long waits for hospital psychiatric attention and medication was restricted to a few drugs with nasty side-effects and uncertain potency. Severely depressed patients were then regular attenders at most GP surgeries. Reluctantly, I reached for the prescription pad and wrote up a powerful anti-depressant, recognising that this was one patient who would be a frequent visitor over months and perhaps years to come.

"Come back and see me in two days," I advised and gave her an extended appointment session and the prescription as I guided her out of the room.

"How is the sleeping?" I asked, as she departed.

"Terrible I don't sleep," she replied which brought my immediate empathy. "We will sort this out," I reassured, although well aware that I had, at best, set up a holding operation. Time was needed for her recovery and to patch up an unhappy initial consultation. She departed, another depressed patient walking the streets with possible intrusive suicidal intent. Suicide appeared to occur with regrettable frequency in these days.

With scarce resources social support was limited at that time and I often worried about the well-being of patients, often living alone, with no external support and thoughts of self-harm. We could only treat where we could and encourage them to live for better days. Many had to live for months and years in abject misery, apathetic and incapable of work or daily living. Miss Whyte was likely to add to their ranks. As I struggled through the rest of the consultations, she slipped from mind until her reappearance a few days later.

I was in more amenable state of mind and conscientiously trying to help attending patients with their physical and psychological problems when she returned.

"I am sleeping better doctor." she said, "Your pills have helped." I was grateful if surprised, for the antidepressant medicine usually took time to become effective.

"I feel brighter." We chatted for some time and I endeavoured to find some solace and therapeutic path for her to cover the time needed for the medicine to kick-in. She was a lonely lady - then labelled a spinster - who had little social contact with men and few interests. Since the death of a supportive mother she had doted upon, she had lived as a recluse in the inherited house surviving on the declining financial estate. I had recently been in one of the psychiatric wards at the local hospital where innovative 'therapy in art' had been launched.

"Healing through art," the posters proclaimed and grasping at straws, I suggested that she might consider doing some art work. She responded very positively.

"My father was an amateur artist and I have often thought I might have a go."

"The very thing I enthused" and suggested I see her in a month to determine any benefit from her prescription.

Off she went and I forgot about her until the month-end when she attended. I was taken aback at her appearance. Gone was the former hair-bun and her appearance was positively Bohemian. Hair was attractively piled up as was the fashion, but she had added a gaudy red ribbon which was off-set by a bright blue scarf at the neck. She had on a sequined, yellow blouse with a short skirt and green tights. Attired like a student, she was certainly making a fashion statement. I was at a loss as to the cause of the transformation. She greeted me effusively.

"I am feeling great doctor. You've really helped me."

"The pills are working then," I said cautiously,

"Oh, I don't know about them, but your idea was brilliant." Now I was floundering, with no idea what she was talking about. "Yes. The art," she burst out, "It's worked like magic. I got some paints and paper and went off to the sea-side for the weekend and it's marvellous. I started to paint and felt better and the more I painted the better I felt. I went home and slept all night. I am hungry again and full of 'Go!' I don't think I need your pills." She said decisively.

Marvelling at this transformation, I cautioned her on too abrupt change of direction, as I had never known the medication to have so quick and dramatic an effect.

"I think we need to keep them going for a bit, maybe at a lower dose," I suggested and she reluctantly agreed to this proposal, before departing for another month.

"Bring some of your painting next visit", I said supportively as she pranced out of the surgery like a frolicking mare rather than a sedate middle-aged matron

A month later she reappeared with several canvasses and euphoric in mood. Her appearance was still more in the role of a bright, young art student. I wondered whether she had in fact been suffering from thyroid disease to account for the dramatic change in attitude, appearance and mood. Blood tests did not confirm this diagnosis. I was forced to assume that the underlying depression had lifted. I was perhaps dealing however with a manic depression and she was perhaps becoming hyperactive.

She proudly presented her pictures which took me aback. Many depressed patients paint dull, dismal, gloomy scenes reflecting their emotive state. Some are lurid, ghostly or abstract renditions. This did not apply to Kate Whyte's work. She had breezily painted coastal villages en plein air and captured the scenes in strong acrylic splashes of colour. They made a statement and attracted the viewer, but their content was less acceptable to my eye. None of the house verticals were straight, horizontals corkscrewed to infinity, chimneys swayed off the perpendicular. The crazy whole somehow, made an attractive picture. They were naïve paintings with a certain charm difficult to define. She was intensely proud of them.

"What do you think? Do you like them?" Cowardly I prevaricated.

"They would certainly look well on some wall somewhere," I suggested, with a garden-shed in mind.

"That is just what I was thinking," she re-joined. "People say they like them and I should show them." Her next words took me aback and I was unprepared for a response. "I was thinking they could go on your waiting-room wall. It's very drab in there and it would brighten the place up."

"It would certainly do that." I stuttered uncertainly. By chance, the partners had discussed hanging paintings on the wall, but I could not imagine their response to her work or its display.

"Good. I shall bring some in". She came back peremptorily and I had lost control of this particular consultation.

"I shall have to ask the partners," I hedged.

"Do that. They'll like them." as she flounced out.

To my surprise, the partners agreed to hang them sight unseen and Kate supervised their placement on the walls. They certainly brightened the interior and were a talking-point for waiting patients, a change from discussion of their ailments and doctors' failings.

Her first sale from the waiting-room exhibits came from one of my patients who had presented with a skin lesion which potentially was cancerous. A skin biopsy was arranged and on return consultation in the surgery he confided,

"You know I quite fancy one of these paintings next door. Who is the artist?" I mentioned the new hobby Kate had taken up. He waited for me to provide the report on his test.

"I am pleased to tell you that the report confirms a simple lesion," I advised. "That is a relief. I am away to buy that picture," he added.

He had determined to buy a picture if the result was negative and the purchase was made to Kate's delight. The space was immediately filled and she began to sell her work. I now rarely saw her as she had discontinued her medication, as neither of us believed it was effective. She was fit and well and full of goodwill and a very different personality than the one who had first come to see me. Both of us were gratified by the transformation.

It was close to Christmas when fate struck. The receptionist reported that the waiting-room walls were bare of paintings. They had mysteriously disappeared. The culprit we suspected was Dougall - a local worthy - who had been waiting for Agnes his itinerant girl-friend at a recent consultation. The police could find no trace of the offender and we consoled Kate at the loss of her work. Her response was blithe,

"I shall just knock up some more and increase my charges. They are selling well," and in due course the paintings were replaced.

We made an insurance claim which was met in full and she received a sizable sum which she used to create an exhibition of her work in the local community centre. The presentation was well-received and was popular with the young. In time. her colourful artwork became collectable and her reputation established. Restored to health, rumbustious and full of bonhomie, I rarely saw her and was saddened when I read of her premature death in a road accident.

A year later my art club held a blind auction of paint materials which had been donated. Only after I had bought paint and brushes did I discover that the source had been Kate's executor. In a bizarre twist of events which had gone full circle, I now owned mementos of a clinical encounter which had started badly but, had a happy therapeutic outcome. Lucky words at the right time had brought success where medication had failed.

Ethical Constraints

The NHS was still in its infancy. Adults recalled the days when they had to pay for doctors' and hospital services and most did not misuse them. My fellow practitioners had been in practice for many years. Each practised in seclusion, with no professional or Governmental intervention, surveillance or audit. There was no special family-doctor training and no health-care staff to assess or criticise quality of care. Patients were accustomed to paternalistic practice, rarely questioned doctors' management and were usually appreciative of the service provided.

There were no booked appointments and waiting-room times could be long, but all patients were seen if they came to surgery and waited. Many resorted to house-call requests that were always honoured. There was no "dragon at the gate" receptionist, or triage nurse filtering off calls to doctors. Patients usually got directly through to the doctor in telephone contacts, or to the long suffering spouse, who juggled at home with the demands of practice and off-spring.

A busy, but routine Monday morning in winter would bring twenty house calls per doctor to be visited that day. Each was also consulting in surgery sessions for three to four hours and often attending patients in the local former Poor Law hospital. Days were long and onerous. Surgery sessions often ran an hour late, as doctors were called out in emergency, while patients patiently waited. House call visits were often trivial, with a scattering of acute cases and many social visits to elderly patients, poorly supported by embryonic social services. In the frequent influenza epidemics, we were swamped by the house-call demand, but would sill honour every visit request and return exhausted in late evening.

Treatment was very dependent on a handful of effective preparations. There was a tiny drug compendium with a few medications for heart and respiratory ailments. As a rural practitioner, I dispensed many simple remedies. Messy ointments had often to be concocted manually on a dispensing slab. Pills were counted singly into small jars and packets. Penicillin and sulphonamides were the only antibiotics, with the former usually given by injection. Disposable equipment had yet to be invented and much time was given to sterilising needles and syringes and surfaces.

The doctor's office was bereft of dressing room, or cubicle and patients disrobed in the corner beside the un-curtained examination couch. Chaperones existed in name only, with doctors and patients only protected by trust and status. Complaints were rare, litigation almost unknown and there was respect, trust and rapport between most patients and doctors, a situation existing over my years in practice. Most doctors believed in offering a good care service to patients and tried to deliver quality care, albeit in an authoritarian and paternalistic fashion.

Patients with terminal conditions, or with cancer, were not routinely apprised of their condition. Spouses might be advised of the situation, but were just as likely to kept in the dark, for their own "protection" in the eyes of the professional. When there was time, the afflicted usually became aware of the prognosis but did not discuss it. Doctor and patient shared a covert understanding that this was so, without overt acknowledgement of the status quo. Surgery was usually the only remedy for cancer. It often only bought time and not cure. Chronic bronchitis, silicosis, debilitating heart disease and crippling arthritis affected many older house-bound people, with only limited means for alleviating symptoms. Professional challenges, although demanding, brought their own rewards with work-satisfaction even on the worst day of work-overload.

Male partners - female GPs. were rare - met occasionally and policy decisions were often made by a parsimonious senior partner resistant to change and expense. In a monumental struggle to upgrade shoddy and unhygienic work spaces in our town surgery, in frustration one day, I blurted out,

"I'll do it myself! "and stalked out of the meeting. Caught out by my petulance, my next weekend was spent tackling office walls with paint brush and distemper, as partners continued to resist renovation and innovation.

Change came slowly. The first mobile telephone to appear was greeted with great excitement for it promised emancipation. The 'on-call' doctor no longer needed to remain close to landlines. I had a love/hate relationship with the contraption It was the size of four bricks and appeared to weigh the same as I lugged it from car to patient.

"Where have you a spare electric socket?" became the first enquiry on a house call. The urgent requirement was to plug in the phone for recharging, as charge lasted only twenty minutes. It defied imagination that powerful successors would ultimately weigh a few grams, be cupped in the hand and hold charge for many hours.

One of the most revolutionary changes, which saved much time and pain and dramatically reduced infection, was the appearance of disposable syringes and latterly dressing and instrument packs. For many years I dismantled reusable metal and glass syringes and their needles, to wash them, clean and sharpen the needles and sterilise them in an autoclave, or pan of hot water, before reassembly. An onerous chore, inevitably, bent and distorted needles would slip through the screen only to be noticed as the solution was being injected into the skin. It was tempting to proceed with the injection to save time in seeking and sterilising a new needle. Blunt and hook-tipped needles resulted in painful injections. Many patients had needle phobias in a time when most antibiotics were given by injection. Uncaring doctors and nurses injected with imperfect needles. I usually resisted this temptation.Cursing inwardly I would lose time discarding and acquiring a sharp needle, priding myself in giving a painless injection to ensure a grateful patient. Once however resolve weakened.

A Needling Event

Abe Driver was the local urban traffic warden. He had been a Warrant Officer in the army and must have been a fearsome tyrant to his men. He proved to be an aggressive, unyielding terror on the streets of Harborough. I suspected him to be a wife-beater, Winnie his subservient wife occasionally arrived in surgery with a blackened eye.

"I walked into a broom handle in the dark," or, "I slipped on the carpet and fell against the door" she would explain, if questioned.

He was punctilious in observing the rule-book while on the job and allowed no deviation in the application of regulations to the unfortunate motorist. He was regularly seen with a ruler measuring the inches a car-bumper overhung a white line. A hefty, florid man who liked his beer, he pounced on the deviant motorist with pleasure and brooked no pleas for mercy and mitigation. He had found his forte and enjoyed booking the unfortunate.

As doctors we had no special dispensation excluding us from road regulations and no reserved parking-bays at the surgery. By custom the 'Doctor' sign in the car-window was normally acknowledged by traffic-wardens. Most applied a blind eye to illegal parking on town house-calls, except for Fred. He saw us as fair game. I had several vocal, verbal encounters with him. Excuses for misconduct were to no avail and the inevitable entry into his book followed.

"Over the line again Doctor." he would announce with barely suppressed glee.

"Just a quick house-call." I would blurt out defensively.

"Three inches over the line," he followed with finality, showing the offending measure on his ruler.

"It was an urgent call," I would insist.

"Against Regulations," he would retaliate, bringing out his book and start paper-work and the battle was lost. Local magistrates and the police invariably looked benignly on these transgressions, but the officious Abe's 'booking' meant hassle, backroom interventions, time-wasting. My ire at his uncompromising and bullying behaviour mounted with the years.

I was running late and time-pressured when Fred appeared in the consulting-room one evening clutching a letter. He had been referred by the local venereologist who had gone on holiday. He ran what was euphemistically called the 'Special clinic' in these days. This catered for venereal disease cases. To encourage people to attend and seek treatment and retain anonymity, conventional referral and management procedures did not apply. Normally we had no cognisance of patients attending the consultant. I occasionally 'stood in' for this professional when he was away however, and met some of his clients.

Fred, taken aback to find I was the acting locum, lost much of his bluster and was obviously apprehensive and far from belligerent.

"Had a busy day?" I said malevolently. "Lots of bookings?"

He unhappily handed over the letter. With unholy glee, I read that Fred had been dallying with a local prostitute and had been infected with gonorrhoea. He was to have ten days of penicillin injections.

"Ten days treatment." I said with a degree of sadistic pleasure.

"I don't like needles," he replied glumly.

"You need ten injections," maliciously "and they are big doses which can be painful." Fred crumpled before my eyes.

"I am really scared of needles. Can't I have pills? Can I not be treated at the hospital?"

"No pills." I said decisively. It's against the rules. You wouldn't want me to break the regulations would you?" Miserably Fred watched as I prepared the syringe, antibiotic ampoule and needle. I did not consciously select an imperfect needle. It may have been a Freudian slip, but as the needle-tip contacted his bare shoulder, I realised that it had been damaged and had a slight hook at its end. I should have abandoned the procedure and sought a new needle, but in a moment of rancour, I plunged it into the skin.

The blunt-end failed to pierce the epidermis and the skin dimpled with the pressure, then the point burst through the surface and in to the deeper tissue. I injected the mixture which distended the tissues and stretched pain-endings, which caused quite a painful experience at any time. Fred wailed and I felt guilty, but had now no choice of action. With-drawing a hooked needle-tip was much more painful than its entry. I genuinely tried to alleviate the pain of withdrawal as it clawed its way back to the surface, without much success. Fred was a wimp. He may have been brave in battle in his Warrant Officer days in the army but his courage deserted him in the surgery and he howled as the needle was retrieved.

"Only another nine to go." I said, guilt overshadowed by memories of our unpleasant street side encounters.

He returned abjectly, the next day, fearful of a repetition of the previous events. In the interim I had struggled with a guilty conscience. Professional ethics had won the day. He had the remaining injections from a pristine needle and went on his way. We continued to meet irregularly when he was patrolling the streets, but there were no more bookings. His condition - perhaps divine retribution - seemed to have resulted in a blind eye to my minor traffic transgressions.

Some years later the surgery receptionist advised that Fred wanted to see me and I thought his benevolence had been exhausted. Apologetically he announced.

"I have just had a look at your car on the street."

"It's only just over the line," I said defensively thinking we were back to the bad old days.

"No. No. That's not the problem. Your registration is two months out of date. I thought I should warn you that you should get it renewed." Mouth agape, I thanked him for his consideration and marvelled at the effect a hooked needle could have on entrenched behaviour.

Bizarre encounter

As a rural doctor, I lived in a geographically close relationship with patients who often became friends. I had to keep professional and neighbourhood relations apart. Relationships could become strained however if cheek by jowl proximity brought over-familiarity with neighbours' life styles and peccadillos. On an 'off-duty' day escaping the cares of the practice, I was tramping in the countryside exercising Hirta my Sheltie collie and blessing the good fortune that had brought residence in such a beautiful area of Scotland. The moors were tinged with russet and gold in the sunlight of a perfect late autumn afternoon.

Chatting with Ed, my walking buddy, we wended a way along the river-side and on to the hill ridge leading to cliffs which girdled the still waters of a lochan. Shattered remnants of a glacial past, the slopes hosted finger-like pinnacles and crumbling buttresses which stood guardian over an eye-entrancing vista of rolling uplands. Chatting amiably and climbing steadily, we advanced with scant regard to trail, through scattered birch trees into a fringe of sombre conifers crowding to the cliff-edge. This was a rarely walked area and we were two miles from the nearest habitation and several from the nearest township.

The route was pathless, spruces guarded the way ahead and we scrambled, some distance from the boundary cliff edge, over rocks, mosses, bracken and heather, intent on conversation rather than upward progress. Above gullies which plunged to the valley floor, there were little verdant mini-alps hidden from lakeside view, or casual passer-by. This was the occasional abode of the itinerant vagrant. I had once or twice come across their makeshift refuges consisting of a few scraps of polythene supported by a bough or two. Otherwise this was a rarely frequented wilderness given over to the patrolling buzzard and hill fox.

As we thrust out of a particularly dense matting of overgrown heather and a tangled, torsion of evergreen branches, Hirta dashed off towards the cliff face, ignoring commands to come to heel. Fearing for his safety, we followed his excited barks. Emerging from the mini-jungle, we suddenly came upon the dog sniffing curiously at a camouflaged bivouac tent. Its presence was incongruous. It was pitched perilously close to the cliff edge and a 100 metre vertical drop, on a perch exposed to strong westerly winds which blasted the cliffs. As we stumbled on this intrusion, I tripped over a guy rope, shaking the fabric and almost diving through a tent wall, This intimate invasion should have brought an irate response from any occupant, but all remained silent.

The refuge appeared abandoned and I wondered what wanderer had chosen such an exposed perch. I conjectured idly,

"Who owns this? It's likely to be blown away if the wind gets up," and Ed conjectured,

"Maybe the owner has fallen over the edge!" and jokingly, "It's a blot on the landscape. We should chuck it over the cliff!"

This idle remark brought a dramatic response, for a tousle-haired head was abruptly thrust through the side opening of the tent door. Too my surprise, I recognised the owner of the flushed, disembodied face which stared upward. Our abrupt appearance must have been a rude shock to him, as was his sudden appearance below to us. The likelihood of any intrusion into this remote all but impregnable spot was unlikely. The chance that it would be by an acquaintance must have been a million to one. The unforeseen blunder into the tent must have been a heart-stopping event for an occupant intent on seduction.

The face belonged to a local lawyer James Stillwell-Worth who I occasionally met socially. His double barrelled name was a reflection of his self-perceived social standing. He belonged to the County set, joining their shooting parties and tennis games. He believed himself a cut above more ordinary village mortals. A practice patient, I had occasionally visited the family home when some of the children were ill.

He lived in a crenelated mansion on the edge of town. There were two Bentley cars in the garage. The children went to boarding school and when called to the house to see one, I was welcomed by the maid. I got the impression that her employers would have preferred that I be ushered in by the back door, the tradesman's entrance. A pompous, self–opinionated, man, he was a pillar of rectitude in the community and Chair of the local marriage guidance council. He was wont to pontificate at committees and I had crossed swords with him in verbal conflict. His wife was a large lady who dominated him and the village committees she sat on. A 'Do Gooder" with a very high opinion of herself, she publicly proclaimed her acts of charity at these meetings.

Taken aback at the sudden apparition, I greeted him by name and rather foolishly in the circumstances, formally introduced him to Ed. We towered above him to his disadvantage.

"I'm trying out my son's new tent." He offered ngenuously.

"A good day for it," I returned conversationally. "You have certainly picked a spot with a view."

For a few moments we discussed the inane but safe topic of the weather. He inferred that it was a family member sharing the tent, but events speedily overtook him. To his obvious embarrassment there was an upheaval beside him and his face was joined by another peering upward. His bare-shouldered companion was a pretty young woman who I recognised as one of the area social workers. Blushing, discomfited and shame-faced, he stuttered again,

"We were just trialling the tent." and his blond tent-mate giggled self consciously. To save him further embarrassment, we took a speedy departure, although tempted to ask about the purpose of the trial.

"Nowt so funny as folk." Ed observed laconically as we moved out of ear shot. When we returned to the distant car park much later, James and lady friend were making their separate departures in different cars. Caught, in flagrante delicto, the lawyer had been doubly unfortunate in having his seclusion invaded and his sexual raptures interrupted by an acquaintance. Unlucky chance, or subconscious bravado, had brought his undoing.

I would meet them both again at professional and social meetings and they brazenly ignored the chance encounter. One wondered why they had not chosen a distant motel for clandestine meetings. Their choice of rendezvous seemed bizarre. Perhaps the chance of discovery, however unlikely, had added zest to their sexual frolics. Further encounters with the over-bearing, dominating wife brought some sympathy for him when I remembered his love tryst. Although bound to secrecy, I became aware that our fiery verbal battles were now in the past. He avoided antagonistic conflict, concerned perhaps that his rural assignations might be brought to light.

Brushes with the Law

The rain was torrential and had been for several days. Streams and rivers were swollen and the river Har had burst banks and inundated the riverside area. I was"on-call" duty overnight and did not relish the prospect of venturing in to the deluge to visit patients. The inevitable telephone call came from Harborough police station at midnight.

"There is an incident and we need your medical attendance." Calls from the constabulary tended to bring apprehension. They rarely gave full detail of circumstances and demanded immediate attention. They were also time-logged which discouraged procrastination in response.

The name of a female patient Hilda Cairns was provided with an address of a farm in the hills south of the town. I vaguely remembered the lady and wondered what had happened to her.

"An accident?" I queried.

"No further information," was the reply.

"Where is it exactly? I quizzed the despatcher.

"Hilltop Farm. It's up a track, off the hill road to the moors," was the laconic reply, as the connection was cut preventing further enquiry. Still new to the practice, I had not previously visited this rural area and nocturnal route-finding to calls could prove frustrating. The Russians were constructing embryonic space rockets, but satellite navigation and radio communications were mere imaginations in boys' comic adventure stories. Once away from the home telephone, I would have no further means of communication with anyone unless there was one at the farm and few had the device.

Disconsolately, I set off to meet the request and was soon travelling along single track lanes bereft of sign-posts and leading into the hills. A westerly gale was blasting squalls of water across the windscreen. The tiny screen-wipers of the Renault 4 L car were proving inadequate for the occasion. The vehicle was rocking in the gusts as I snaked further into the hills. Safe driving on the cork-screwing track required good visibility and concentration. Still half asleep, both were in short supply. Coasting downhill and round a bend, I was unprepared for the sudden appearance of a ford and reflexes were slow. A raging stream of water lay ahead. I hit it at speed, with the vehicle's momentum surging the car through the torrent, throwing up huge waves. Braking late, the engine threatened to stall when the vehicle was climbing the opposite incline. Frenzied acceleration brought salvation however.

Now thoroughly awake, I had still failed to identify the track leading to the farm by the road-end some miles away and was forced to retrace my route. In the absence of direction -posts and indicators-deemed an unnecessary expense by frugal hill farmers- twice more, I had to brave the rising stream. Ultimately, I spied a sign which had fallen from its perch and was embedded in the banking. It pointed upwards into the teeth of the gale. The farm track was unfenced, a river of mud and manure, deep rutted, potholed and suited only for a tractor. Patience, never my strong feature, deserted me and I was raging inwardly at the cruel fate that had brought me out on such a foul night.

At last, a dim light heralded the destination. After a perilous plank crossing over a small ravine, I finally reached the patient's abode. A police patrol vehicle was parked in the yard. Descending thankfully from the car, my feet slipped in a watery mess of cow-dung and rotten straw as I crossed the courtyard. Irritated at the police failure to provide adequate route directions, I stomped into the farm, barely controlling my temper. Beyond the vestibule was a small room poorly lit by a paraffin lamp, where I was confronted by a police constable.

"PC. Duguid" he laconically announced, "Next door." The patient was lying abed in an even smaller adjacent room with the same inadequate lighting. I had seen her only once previously in surgery. Her diagnosis had been easy to elicit as she had a swollen, puffy, swelling under the neck, an indication of goitre. Hilda Cairns was a forty year old widow who valiantly strived to run a hill farm after her husband had been killed in a farm accident. A hard working couple they had laboured long, hard hours to earn a living from a poor, upland farm carrying a few cows and scattering of hill sheep. Production of their own brood had been far from easy and after her several miscarriages they had finally produced a much desired daughter who tragically died in child-birth.

Distraught, they had consoled each other, retreating into the isolation of their farm and repressed grief and frustration in an unending battle against unproductive land and a hostile environment. His untimely death, when a tractor overturned, was a dreadful blow to Hilda, who withdrew further from society to lead a solitary existence with her animals on the moors. She had long rejected social support and medical aid until arriving some weeks previously in the village surgery.

On arrival, she was poorly dressed and looked uncared-for, with hair unkempt and hands and nails ingrained with dirt. Hilda's movements and speech were slow and she took a while to consider my questions.

"How are you feeling," I enquired concerned at her appearance. Abjectly apologetic for taking up my time during the consultation, she explained,

"Tiredness and fatigue are making it impossible to tend the farm. I'm falling asleep milking the cows," was slowly announced. There was no complaint of the drudgery or solitude of her existence and she insisted she was fine otherwise. On my concerned enquiry she admitted. "I run the farm on my own."

"No farm hands or relatives to lend a hand," I asked.

"No. I manage myself. I just need something to pep me up doctor. A wee tonic perhaps."

She exhibited many of the signs and symptoms of a malfunctioning thyroid gland and I started her on treatment, took a blood test and arranged follow up appointments, then forgot about her. This was a professionally satisfying diagnosis, for the condition could be treated, unlike many of the day to day problems then presenting in general practice. She was not making enough thyroid hormone, which could be replaced by oral tablets. Hypothyroidism was not easily controlled however and patients often had mood changes, flattened affect and depression which lifted with treatment.

"No I am just tired, "she insisted when asked about her well-being, "although I am not very hungry. If I ate more, maybe I would have more energy."

A month later, Hilda now lay at peace in her tidy bedroom. She had apparently slept her life away. A blessed release perhaps, I wondered. Her clothes were sorted in neat piles on chairs by the bed and a pack of thyroid pills lay on the bedside table with a glass of water. There was nothing untoward in the domestic scene. The cause of her death eluded me as I examined her. Mystified as to the cause of her premature demise, I could not complete a certificate testifying to the cause of death and readied myself to fight my return home against the elements.

Another police officer appeared and announced, "Sergeant Slowcombe." Lugubrious in speech, stolid in movement and unwelcoming in manner, he listened silently to my report and opinion that the procurator fiscal should intervene, a requirement in a sudden unexplained death. The medical cause which had defied me became immediately apparent however when a suicide note, which had lain beside the body, was belatedly produced. An empty bottle labelled 'Sleeping pills' had been found in the kitchen. A partner had apparently prescribed them.

"Slowcombe by name and nature," I thought sourly. If the letter had been presented on my arrival, it would have aided diagnosis. Local Bobbies seemed to anticipate that all sudden deaths had resulted from murder most foul and sought supportive evidence, despite a prima facie contrary conclusion.

"Why did you not give me this when I arrived?" I barked furiously. My justified grievance fell on deaf ears as I headed for the door and back into a particularly vicious squall of rain. Forgetful of the slippery surface, my feet went out from under me and dumped me in malodourous slurry, to further fuel my anger. Wet, cold and angry I returned disconsolately to a cold bed unhappy with the doctor's lot. I had learned the need to negotiate farm yards with care and a determination to actively direct future inter-professional relations with guardians of the law.

Poor Hilda, her overt signs of thyroid disease had masked an underlying depression and I had failed to uncover her suicidal thoughts. She had hoarded barbiturate sleeping pills and taken them all before retiring to bed. Her early death although perhaps welcome, might not have occurred if the thyroid hormone replacement tablets had had time to become effective and lifted her depression and suicidal intent. Further investigation revealed that the farm was insolvent, bankruptcy proceedings were in train and this was a burden the socially isolated women could not bear.

Sudden Death

Police and medical responses were sometimes at odds with emergency calls. A late night call to a former croft house in the Riverside area of Harborough required a walk over a footbridge to a small hamlet snuggling in a loop of the river. The house was a 150 year old croft with tiny rooms. The door from the street led straight in to a small living-room, with very low doors opening into a scullery and minute bedroom. PC Duguid and Jimmie the detective greeted me, convinced that a heinous crime had been perpetrated. The lanky constable was bent almost double as he stooped his head to avoid contact with low ceiling rafters.

"An old woman is dead in the bedroom. A Mrs, McGowan. She lives alone and nobody has seen her for two days," the detective said excitedly and it was apparent that murder was in their minds. The former was a rare event for local constabulary and might bring promotion for investigating officers.

Waved over to the bedroom, I pushed at the ancient, wood-planked door to enlarge the gap further, but it would only open two inches. Leaning forward, I peered through the opened space between door and frame and was slow to realise that I was looking directly into a woman's bare, rear quarters. A patulous gaping vulva guarded by two fleshy white thighs was presented to me and I could understand the policeman's excitement.

"Has she been coshed?" quizzed Jimmy Keen.

Murder and rape were reasonable conclusions. He was to be disappointed however. The explanation was more mundane. Forcing myself with great difficulty past a body in the early stage of rigor mortis, I discovered that far from being accosted physically, she had been preparing for bed. Half-undressed, she had probably suffered a "drop-attack" when the brain was starved of blood and oxygen. Restrained by the narrow precincts of wall and bed, she had fallen forwards towards the floor and her body had been arrested halfway, with her head down between the two. The nightgown had been drawn up over her bottom as she fell forward. Her rear had thrust against the closed door. Unlikely at first view, her posture in death was natural and not subject to suspicious circumstances.

"No, No, she has just died at an unfortunate time and in an unfortunate position," I assured him. "She has had some warning attacks in the past and had a heart problem." She had indeed a history of several cerebral "drop-attacks", when blood to her brain was temporarily impeded and she collapsed. I had been called to see her before, as had partners. The possibility of more attacks was recognised, but no medications were then available to forestall them. Once her body was prostrate, the blood pooled in her lower areas no longer had to struggle against gravity to reach the brain. Brain-flow was re-established and she would recover consciousness. On this terminal occasion her collapsing body had been obstructed by the bed and wall. Her head had remained elevated with resistance to blood flow and oxygen starvation of the brain and death. Jimmy was still keen to initiate a murder investigation.

"It's a procurator case then," Jimmy said hopefully, as he sought to pass the case to the procurator fiscal as an untimely death from natural causes.

"I doubt, he will be interested, "I observed. "I'll have to report it to the DI," said Jimmie.

"I doubt they will want to be involved, " I replied.

In the absence of house break-in or sexual entry his superiors wisely refused to intervene. The episode although bizarre, was treated as a routine death from natural causes.

Jimmie's potential moment of glory was dashed with my diagnosis, but some years later he would attract more public attention than he wished, when embroiled in multiple murders which occurred on his patch.

I continued to have regular encounters with the police force. Once, I had concerns about my personal safety after a call from a patient's husband. Jasper Fortune was a dentist who had developed paranoid behaviour and an unstable personality. Very solidly built and over two metres tall, he had been a boxer in his youth. He had the misfortune to marry an alcoholic lady. Both would physically abuse each other.

Although he did not have a doctorate, he was pompous, belligerent and insisted he be called "Doctor", His associates claimed themselves dental surgeons and stuck with "Mr." in address. My failure to acknowledge his self acclaimed status undoubtedly aggrieved him. Over time, I had had repeated, heated differences of opinion with him regarding his wife's care. In a recent encounter he had come close to physical aggression. He lived in a rather remote country house. For the first and only time in my career, I thought that back-up support might be advisable, if he rang insisting on a visit for a wife in an alcoholic stupor.

"There is nothing I can do for her at this time of night." I stated baldly when he called late one evening.

"I'll give you a good going-over." He threatened, "if you do not come out right away," when I opposed his demand. "Get your arse down here now," he shouted in language more suited to the gutter than a profession. I felt the visit was unjustified and that I could offer nothing for Celia, his whisky-sodden spouse who was usually as verbally abusive as he when in her cups. He continued to shout into the telephone and would brook no delay in response. Tall, weighty and a trained boxer, I suspected he might better me in physical encounter. I cravenly took the line of least resistance and agreed to visit. Aware of a difficult if not hazardous consultation ahead, I rang the local police for support. They assured me a patrol-car would meet me at the house and their officers would control the situation.

The car was indeed there when I arrived and a diminutive policeman and even more petite police woman greeted me. Deferentially the PC. approached and said,

"Doc. We wondered if you would like to make the visit first on your own. We have had dealings with Mr.Fortune before and he gets excited and unmanageable!" Wondering about the valour of modern constabulary, I agreed to make the visit alone, with the officers once again ensconced in their car.

A shouting, aggressive dentist met me at the door

"Get her into hospital," he demanded "I have had enough of her." I felt I also had suffered enough from their inappropriate demands, but stayed silent. The house was in disarray and filthy. Rubbish and clothes were piled everywhere and the obese, inebriated wife lay sprawled across a bed draped with dirty sheets.

This was a social problem and one which could only be resolved with the treatment of the addiction –difficult to arrange with her consent in conventional working hours and certainly insoluble at midnight when she was in an alcohol induced stupor. Social-workers, resistant to work in antisocial hours, were all safely tucked up in bed, so there was no possibility of social care support. The overloaded psychiatric unit would not contemplate such an admission. I refused his entreaties and escaping flying punches and more truculent demands to have her forcibly removed to hospital, escaped at speed back to my car. The waiting police constable announced sheepish, "I thought he might be violent!"

The two police officers then distanced themselves from the impending fracas within the security of their transport and radioed for backup support. Fortune continued to threaten vengeance and long remained a personal threat to my wellbeing. Practice remuneration was then dependent on per capita patient income and thrifty partners would never exclude a patient from the practice list. In time Celia drank herself to death and he later hanged himself in an act little regretted by the community.

Unexpected outcome

Another police call via PC. Duguid's radio brought better cooperation and a more joyous outcome. He had been visiting a farm where there had been a cattle-rustling incident.

"I am at Manor Farm. I need you doctor. I think Mrs. Plowright is having a baby," he added. The worthy PC. Duguid had four children of his own and I felt he should be familiar with pregnancy and childbirth. In this instance I could understand his reservation however. I had visited Pete Plowright's farm to see John an ailing eleven year old son a few months previously. The lady of the house had not been overtly pregnant, nor had she been attending the ante-natal clinic. I further questioned the village policeman who had recently taken up rural duties.

"Have you got the right name? We do not have any pregnant women on the farm. She says she is not pregnant and the husband agrees, but it looks like a baby's head and there is a lot of blood and the ambulance is fifteen miles away. You need to come at once please." He pleaded.

Grabbing the midwifery bag, I rushed through the lanes to the nearby village of Colton and the farm. On arrival at her house, young John was playing in the yard,

"Mums got a sair belly," he advised as I passed his swing. Pete the farmer met me at the door.

"She can't be pregnant, he vouchsafed, she has just got a bit fat."

I entered the bed-room to find a very flushed Andy Duguid valiantly holding a towel over an imminent vaginal delivery. Emily Plowright a solidly built woman in her mid-forties, was lying across the bed loudly proclaiming between abdominal pains.

"I can't be pregnant. John is 11 now." While still denying the possibility of imminent birth, a paroxysm of abdominal pain overcame her. Then in anguish, "I am not pregnant, doctor," and with less certainty from the bewildered new mother to be, "just don't have periods." I examined the distended vulva and observed an already partially delivered baby's head.

"Push." I ordered the reluctant mum who continued to strenuously deny possible child birth. Push she did and within a few minutes a lusty infant was born and I delivered a healthy baby girl.

"Get a drawer from the chest," I instructed Andy who was also coming to terms with the delivery. He phlegmatically emptied a drawer from a clothes chest and lined it with cotton-wool to cot the new-born. As I placed the baby in her arms, a befuddled father was still disputing Emily's changed status.

"She is just putting on weight." he averred, while mum was coming to terms with the new birth.

"Well she has just lost 9lbs." I observed facetiously.

"I thought I was just getting fat Pete," she said in shocked disbelief as he made his appearance and they struggled to accept the sudden doubling of the family. Suspecting the menopause, she had spent her pregnancy in self-denial, with husband and relatives believing only that she had been gaining weight.

At the post-natal clinic Emily rather shame-facedly said,

"I just thought at first my increased size was due to fat. Then later, I worried I had a growth and was frightened to have it seen to." She had remained oblivious to the possibility of pregnancy to the point of delivery. The baby was none the worse for this unexpected arrival, but it took dad and mum much longer to recover psychologically from the experience.

A Speeding Offence

My personal brushes with the law were put in perspective a few months later when my presence at an outlying village was urgently requested at 2am. Half asleep, I sped along the trunk road to the destination. Foot down on the accelerator on an empty road and with thoughts on the patient, I was travelling far over the posted speed limit. A car sped up from behind however and as it overtook, I was startled to see it was a police vehicle. For a few moments, we drove along side. Convinced I was about to be booked for speeding. I astutely lifted the stethoscope lying on the seat beside me and dangled it in front of the side window. The police officer in the passenger seat responded with alacrity by suspending his handcuffs to view!

His car drew ahead and I prepared to be pulled over and be booked, but it increased speed and sped ahead as I belatedly adhered to the legal speed limit. I expected to see his car in ambush round the next bend or at the next lay-by. However it was not in sight and I relaxed a little as the miles went by, thinking I had escaped a fine. Approaching a point where the neighbouring canal met with the road at a bridge however, the inevitable blinking blue lights commanded a stop.

The patrol vehicle half-blocked the roadway and the police-man with the handcuffs was standing by. I recognised him as husband of one of my patients.

"Give you a fright doc.?" He grinned.

"I'm on my way to an emergency," I stuttered defensively, waiting for the booking.

"We recognised your car. On you go, but take care. You were going at a fair lick. We are looking for a prisoner who escaped and ran off along the canal." I drove off thankfully blessing good fortune. Some weeks later the pc's wife attended surgery and I mentioned meeting her husband.

"Yes," she acknowledged with smile. "Brian said that we could rely on you getting to us fast if we ever needed you in a hurry!" The sight of the dangling hand-cuffs lodged in my memory, but the scales of justice had swung in my favour. This was one family that could expect a prompt response to their calls, when in need.

Musical Interludes

Mrs Addie Pose waddled in to the consulting room and spread herself across the rather inadequate consulting room chair, her vast thighs overhanging the seat by a considerable margin. She was a very large lady weighing close to twenty stones and all my inducements to have her lose weight went in vain. Her obesity caused many health problems which brought her regularly to surgery. She could not accept that adiposity was the root cause of her ill health. After many verbal conflicts attempting to have her restrict food consumption I lost the battle of wills. She loved fizzy drinks and potato crisps and would undoubtedly, in my opinion, go to her maker clutching a coke can and crisp packet. She did enliven her visits however with her quaintly worded requests.

"I have a confection in the ear" she once confessed and I wondered what dietary advice was appropriate here. "Nurse put an anemone up me", she confided, after having been administered an enema. I momentarily considered that the nurse had been in playful mood. "Can I please have a self-inflicted sick line", was a standard request as she ended each consultation. I had to resist writing "obesity" as the diagnosis on the sickness certificate. An accurate description, I chickened out of a confrontation and lamely wrote "venous insufficiency" to explain her grossly distended legs.

"Can I have something for piles before I go," she added and I was tempted to offer a pile-driver.

"I need something for cold feet" she demanded one day and I could not resist the temptation,

"Socks." I offered, but the attempt at humour was lost upon her. She was slightly hard of hearing which further challenged our communications. She crossly accused me one day that I had failed to tell her she had AIDs. I was at a loss to follow her condemnation, as I found it hard to believe that a man would get physically close enough to her vast bulk to be intimate and infect her.

"The nurse told me," she angrily announced. Discreet questioning finally revealed that the district nurse had visited her at home enquiring about mobility aids!

To establish rapport with patients I sought information on hobbies and pastimes before exploring the reason for patients' consultations, which they were often reluctant to reveal. The, 'While I am here doctor' interjection at the end of the consultation was one I tried to avoid, as I then over-ran appointment times.

Gardening was often an introductory topic of conversation, the common ground between patient and doctor, which established empathy before weighty medical matters were discussed.

"How are you? How is the garden?" was my introduction to many consultations, which brought pithy comment on lilies, broccoli and carrots, all of interest to the rural gardener. Willy Comfort was a keen gardener winning many prizes in the annual competitions and we embarked on the usual description of his vegetables when he arrived for a consultation. He had been a miner and reported he was occasionally short of breath. The conversation reminded me yet again that the patient/doctor relationship was often a two- way process of benefit to patient and doctor. My patient contacts had over the years brought colour and enlightenment to my life.

We chatted about his rheumatism and his belief that a proprietary product called 'Wintergreen' balm worked wonderfully for him. Then came the inevitable,

"While I'm here doctor" followed by, "I really struggle for breath on warm sultry, damp days." I checked his chest with the stethoscope and found signs of 'miner's lung'. The condition was not too advanced, although it caused the death of many miners. There was no specific treatment for silicosis and I reassured him. Then he said casually,

"Mind you, it does not interfere with playing the pipes."

He played the Highland bagpipes and this revelation stimulated my personal interest. I had a liking for music-making. I had aspired to pay the bugle in the Boy Scout band, but pursed lips and puffed cheeks brought only discordant screeches. This ensured I was dumped in the percussion section by fellow players. There, I discovered a talent for missing the beat and was relegated to carrying the parade banner, where the only requirement was to keep step.

The gift of a push-button harmonica prior to National Service 'call-up' inspired further musical effort in the barracks, to the ire of fellow combatants. Efforts to master the instrument only resulted initially in an off-key rendition of the national anthem. An expanding musical repertoire did finally encourage accompaniment to barrack-room ditties. Later time-constrained academia had quashed musical leanings until I took up the saxaphone.

Domicile in a border village brought a latent patriotism to the fore however. I developed a yearning for the Highland bagpipe and traditional dance. Anne and I joined a Scottish Country Dance Club to integrate with the local musical community. Clad in shirt, flannels and ancient plimsolls, I presented to the class, secure in the fond belief that passing acquaintance with the pas de bas gained at school when performing an impromptu sixteen - some reel - would stand me in good stead in this unsophisticated rural setting. We were greeted, in broad Welsh vernacular by a gentleman impeccably attired in Highland evening dress.

Mr. Jones was a practice patient. A former Welsh guardsman, tall and imposing in stature, he took his tutoring duties very seriously.

"You will be joining the introductory class Doctor," he suggested in a sonorous Welsh accent untainted by the local idiom, despite 30 years of living in the Borders. Inevitably known as Taff, he was a local forester and his command of Scottish Country Dance steps was beyond reproach. The class performed meticulously under his command, took earnest delight in perfectly portraying strathspeys and jigs and showed disdain for my wild whoops of animal delight as I whirled unceremoniously through reels. Suitably chastened, I returned to the next class, clad in the kilt and clutching a dance instruction book.

Willy's words brought a thoughtless response and I revealed that,

"I have long yearned to play the pipes." Willy immediately encouraged my interest.

"Niver too old to have a go", he alleged. "I'll gi ye a haund wi' the learning o' thim." He offered.

His words encouraged acquisition of a set of bagpipes. I glanced wistfully at advertisements for silver- mounted, blackwood-stocked and ivory-embellished instruments at inflated prices and started hunting local junk-shops and street markets. Poor Willy unfortunately, was overtaken by a fulminating pneumonia during a flu epidemic, which resisted antibiotic treatment. One of his last acts before he died was to obtain a set of bagpipes and post them to me.

Their arrival fulfilled a cherished dream, one which soon became a protracted nightmare resulting in a love/hate relationship lasting a lifetime. Of all the instruments ambition had tempted me to play, - this bag of wind and its wailing drones brought me nearest to howling insanity - a state to which Sassenach listeners are occasionally reduced when hearing them. They exhibit some unappealing characteristics, being fickle, unreliable and unresponsive on occasion. They require prolonged courtship, gentle handling and can respond to tender love and fondling with a magnificent performance. Some brave sexist souls have likened the relationship to that of man and woman

Without Willie's anticipated assistance, frustrating days of struggle followed their arrival. The opened parcel revealed what purported to be a bagpipe set in its component parts. I attempted to assemble pieces which refused to conform in basic structure to my preconceptions of the instrument. I endeavoured to assemble the host of tubes, ivories, ferrules, reeds and braids and fix them into a rustic bag clothed in disreputable tattered tartan. For days I tried to assemble them in every conceivable and inconceivable combination, without success. Either there were too many fitting orifices in the bag or too few and always, bits of wood and ivory would remain to mock me. Finally a frenzied call to the donor's son revealed that the miscellany were remnants of several instruments.

Misconceived from birth, the vitals had come from many discarded bagpipes bequeathed by a disbanded pipe-band after their headquarters had been almost obliterated by fire. The assembled set would lie arachnoid-like upon the floor, invariably an appendage short or sporting an extra limb. Resisting my best endeavours, it would writhe under my grasp as I wrestled yet again to reassemble misfitting parts. At last, however, with aid of hammer and chisel, the deed was done. Satisfied with the anatomy I turned to a study of its physiology. I tried vainly to blow some life into the dormant bag and found the creature to be mute. Huff and puff as I might, no cajoling, coercion or cursing of that desiccated vestige of sheep gut would induce it to inflate. In desperation I bought a bagpipe tutor book and there on the first page the terrible truth was told:

"It takes seven years and seven generations to make a bagpipe player." I believed every word! The days of assembly were followed by weeks of pulmonary effort, with the beast still to be tamed. It resolutely refused to utter a single sound if one discounts an occasional despairing groan or sneering hiss. The reeds I ultimately found were so hard and inflexible, that only the energy needed to blast sound through a factory whistle would have moved them. A desperate attack with sand-paper brought improvement, but sound emissions were far from encouraging, although effective in scaring off neighbourhood cats.

The resolve of lesser men would have faltered, but Celts are made of stern stuff and I turned to the practice-chanter. A long-suffering wife listened to my initial efforts and threatened separation, divorce, or worse, so I retired to the relative seclusion of my surgery premises after hours. I wondered if the eldritch sounds escaping from this place of employment were thought by passers-by to be emanating from a lingering soul lost in anguish - the office was opposite an undertaker's premises! In time - a very long time - my performance became a little more melodious, at least to the untutored ear. I resolved to face the bagpipe monster again. This was a painful transition accompanied by the bursting of balloon-size bullae in protesting lungs, as I tried vainly to blow some life into the dormant bag. It leaked like a sieve. I poured generous portions of syrup, molasses, lubricant and finally, even whisky into its ungrateful maw without appeasing the creature. Recognising defeat it had to be discarded, or salvation sought elsewhere.

Venturing north to Edinburgh's Royal Mile and the shop of a bagpipe maker. A little, stooped, wizen - faced, ancient piper cast eyes upon my purchase. I unwrapped the prized and nurtured acquisition. Startled, he exclaimed,

"Goad. 'I've niver seen the like. Where did ye git this laddie? Aff the midden? That bag will niver haud its wind. It's fu' o' holes."

Chagrined at his response, I despaired that a playing set of bagpipes would ever be mine. The old man rose to the challenge however and I exchanged the desiccated old bag for a new model made of Gore-Tex material, which never needed nutritional placation and could be inflated by an eight-year-old.

Now at last it seemed I could face my public, if such there was. Even Hirta my dog's loyalty was suspect as he was wont to howl in apparent anguish, the moment the chanter was placed to my lips. Success still eluded me, for neglected reeds objected noisily to their long inactivity.A dreadful cacophony fell upon the unsuspecting ear, as I ventured on my first melody. Impervious to these strident screams of protest, I took up practising in an ancient barn on the hill above home. It gained local notoriety with a reputation of being haunted, when discordant practice notes leaked beyond the walls and wafted across mist enveloped fields to frighten nocturnal walkers.

Gradually, the brute was tamed and one wild Hogmanay I ventured at last into the public eye, choosing a pub full of revellers for my debut. Suitably fortified for the occasion and breathing alcoholic fumes liberally into the bag, my performance was greeted rapturously by an intoxicated audience. Euphoria was soon dissipated however when a similar rendition was performed before a retired pipe major.

Geordie was another practice patient – as were all the village residents. He had been a shepherd. Well into his eighties he was now crippled with arthritis and called in for a consultation about his ailment. His gnarled hands and bent fingers still lovingly caressed the chanter when he was playing at village ceilidhs and I admired his dexterity with grace notes, which I had yet to master. He was taciturn by nature and a man of few words, after a life of solitary living in the wilds.

"Aye, I'll hae a listen laddie," he responded when I suggested he might give an opinion of my new musical skills. He listened for a few minutes with an expression of disbelief, while I gave the tune my best shot,

"Bluidy unbelievable!" followed by several expletives which allowed no misinterpretation of his feelings, then "I'll awa then," and he was off, never to discuss my debacle again.

Disconsolate I retired to lonely country spots for further practice. Seclusion was rarely possible for, heifers and bullocks from far afield would hearken to the first note of the Great Pipe. Surrounding me they would snort, slobber and paw the ground making what I hoped were playful charges. At least, they appeared to enjoy the repertoire, though local farmers maintained that my playing decreased egg-laying performance of their hens!

James McLaren a Regimental Pipe major moved into the village and on to my practice list. He magnanimously offered tuition and I would present before him to have all my wayward musical habits reconditioned. Treated as his most recalcitrant recruit, I feared each tutorial encounter, but slowly became a piper. By the seventh year of acquaintance with my set of pipes, a precarious rapport had been established. The bagpipe, I had come to realise, possesses female attributes, being often unreliable, unpredictable and invariably fickle. The instrument has to be humoured, nurtured and cherished. Like a woman it responds occasionally to a gentle caress or may prefer to have contours hugged close to a manly chest. Gripped firmly it can be mastered and enticed into memorable performance, but taken unawares and unprepared the response can be disappointing.

My pipes showed marked distaste for the cold and either refused to strike up or shrieked disapproval, if exposed to low temperatures. They would stubbornly play off-key if inadequately prepared for musical interlude, and then the audience would respectfully, or more frequently menacingly, request that I played the refrain "Far Away". The instrument also disliked getting wet and drones would suddenly cut out and throw marchers out of step if I was leading a parade. As in the female wont, weddings were always favoured. In a gaily turned-out ensemble, with ribbons fluttering in the breeze, the piping rendition was always faultless.

Hogmanay festivities were also welcomed and one could be sure then of a spirited if sometimes wanton performance. Once, my complete repertoire of dubious musical merit was recorded for oriental posterity by an eager Japanese tourist festooned with camera and tape-recorder accessories. This misguided Asian may, have been tone deaf, inebriated with saki, or seeking a recording to frighten the birds off his rice crops.

I no longer looked upon my fiendish instrument of torture as a musical liability but a future financial asset, as ivory continued to increase in value. Bronchitis, intermittent wheeze and lungs bulging with bullae can be sad testimony to prolonged, passionate sessions with the 'bag o' wind.' 'Bagpipers' Disease has been recognised and the causative fungus carried off a stalwart New Zealand piper. Scottish pipers are believed to be immune to this terrible malady, as whisky fumes are reputed to kill all the organisms which inhabit their bagpipes. All those who would dally with the Great Highland Bagpipe should perhaps be forewarned of the dangers of potential terminal addiction.

Contrasting Personalities

Angela apologised as she entered, as was her wont. She had become a regular surgery visitor when work-stress had triggered an upset stomach, which had settled into an annoying irritable bowel disturbance. After an adventurous Asian holiday, she had previously suffered a prolonged intestinal problem. In some people this event can trigger recurring gut spasms and diarrhoea. In most people, this is an annoyance and rarely life-threatening. However, Angela's intestinal upset had become chronic and diagnosed as irritable syndrome (IBS). I was concerned that cancer of the bowel, sometimes associated with the condition, might occur.

"I'm sorry to bother you Doctor. It's a minor complaint and you are so busy." She was a tall, willowy, natural blond and strikingly good-looking, I had met her occasionally when wearing my other hat as attending doctor at the local geriatric unit. A physiotherapist very dedicated to her work, she did treatment sessions with stroke victims and was popular with patients and staff. I admired her natural rapport with the elderly, her cheerful demeanour and encouragement to those suddenly faced with crippling, physical disability. Aged in her early fifties, she had recently severed a long relationship with a male partner and was now living on her own in a house over-looking the river Har.

"It's always a pleasure to see you" I said sincerely, words which did not apply to all my patients. "How is the IBS?"

"I am coping." She responded.

On questioning however, it was apparent that her bowel condition was a serious concern. I changed some of her medication hoping to improve her symptoms. Always appreciative of my management, she lingered before leaving.

"While I am here doctor," and I waited for the revelation. "This really is a silly little thing to bother you with." she apologised.

"What is worrying you?" I encouraged.

"Well, it is a funny tingling sensation round my mouth and up to my right eye. It only lasts a few seconds. I hope I am not wasting your time."

"Oh, there can be several simple reasons for this." I assured her, reassured from the description that this was a minor occurrence. "How often have you had it?"

"Just two or three times in the last few days. It seems to happen at any time and lasts a few minutes."

There were several diagnostic possibilities, most benign and self-limiting. This sounded like a mild nerve disturbance, although some of these could be tiresome and long lasting. The change in sensation she mentioned could involve the facial nerve, which ran from the brain to the jaw, through a narrow bone canal in the cheek. If there was swelling of bone or nerve, sensation and feeling could be altered, or pain occur. I hoped that there was nothing serious. As GPs, we saw many sparrows in the diagnostic field and canaries were rare. Our training however encouraged anticipation of the malign and consideration of less likely eventualities. With thoughts on more likely simple causes I asked,

"Any trouble with the teeth?"

"No, they get checked regularly."

"No recent mouth, face, jaw infections?"

"No."

"Any changes in your medications?" I mused, glancing at her notes to confirm my memory. "No other virus infections, bites or anything unusual?"

"No, nothing. I am quite fit. I hill-walk, ski and play squash," she then affirmed.

I quickly tested the facial nerves to ensure there was no change in sensation and feeling in jaw and face. Nerve reflexes were all normal, so then I suggested,

"Perhaps you could have your dentist check your teeth again." I wondered if a facial neuralgia, or herpes zoster virus, which causes shingles, might be threatening. Satisfied that this was some minor aberration, I reassured her and sent her off with the usual proviso,

"If it becomes worse and does not settle shortly, come in and see me again." Then as an afterthought for a favoured patient,

"Tell reception they have to fit you in at any time". I cheered her on her way and forgot the pleasant interview completely, as the grossly overweight Mrs. Addie Pose heaved through the door to start a further tiresome, tedious difficult consultation.

This vast ladies' bulk overfilled and overhung the consulting-room chair. She was a weekly attender who always overran her appointment and considered my time at her personal disposal. She was a poseur, complainer and whinged on about simple complaints invariably related to her girth and adiposity. She suffered from high blood pressure, osteoarthritis, kidney problems and diabetes, all related to her gross obesity and steadfastly refused to consider any suggestion to restrict her diet or food intake.

"Running late again!" She burst out belligerently and my heart sank at the verbal battle about to ensue, as I tried to manage her many clinical conditions. Our animosity was mutual and she ought to have moved on to a more amenable clinician. I defied her demands for weight-loss pills and sleeping medication, neither of which I thought were in her best interest.

"What's the problem today," as I prepared to placate her.

"It's my gastric stomach," she would usually accost me crossly, pointing vaguely at the great pendulous mass that over-flowed her lap above vast thighs. 'Mountainous stomach', I always thought wryly was a more appropriate definition for a gross appendage.

"It's my legs. They are killing me. They are twice the size they once were. What are you going to do about it?" This I felt was an under-estimate of their girth and I wondered how she could tell. So vast was her bulk that I doubted she could see beyond the great superstructure of a bosom, supported by grossly distended abdomen and thighs capable of supporting an oak tree. The surgery scales spun out of control under her weight and would not accurately register her monstrosity. Clinic-staff probably guessed her weight.

Once again for the umpteenth time, I started down the long road of explanation about cause and effect and the need to restrict a diet which was mainly, fish, chips, cakes and lemonade. She launched into her usual tirade reiterating,

"I barely eat a thing," her voice rising with each word! "I need stronger water pills," She was convinced that medicines could correct all her problems, I longingly thought of the quick consultation that had gone before.

Twenty minutes later, to conclude the verbal battle which I had inevitably lost, I slightly modified her medicine regimen then prised and heaved Addie out of her seat and towards the door. Relieved that a further week would pass before she reappeared on the scene, I was tempted to suggest a return in a month, but knew she would create a scene in the waiting-room reception, until a battle-scarred receptionist gave in to her demands. Her blood-pressure and sugar levels were dangerously high and her diabetes and heart status a serious concern, but she adamantly refused to contemplate any personal measures to alleviate her condition. Self-centred and self- indulgent Addie Pose was undoubtedly going to succumb to her multiple, weight-related conditions at a relatively young age.

As she left, I reflected for a moment on the two recent consultations and the contrast in personal attitudes. One patient was a giver and the other a taker. Further divergent behavioural characteristics in contrasting personalities would unfold in weeks to come, In two proximal but disparate consultations, one was self-inflicted and the other a bolt from the blue.

Two days later Angela was back having been fitted in urgently between consultations. Apologetic as always she started,

"I am really sorry to bother you again, but my jaw seems to quiver, then I lose sensation in my mouth. My work colleague says she saw my eye-lid drop. It has happened three times since I saw you." She was obviously worried. I was now seriously concerned about the underlying condition and wondered about a diagnosis of Lyme disease, which can come from a tick-bite. Ticks are common in Scottish hill lands. The condition can have weird neurological presentations. A drooping eye-lid and nerve disturbance to one side of the face sometimes happens with the infection.

"When you are out on the hills have you had any tick-bites?" I asked.

"A few times, but nothing recently. I always check for bites after walks. I know they can carry disease," she replied.

"Never any rashes after bites?" I further queried. A circular skin inflammation, known as a 'herald patch,' often appeared on the skin a few days after a tick-bite. This was a sign that Lyme disease and later nerve complications could arise – sometimes months after the bite.

"No, never," she said decisively.

A quick neurological examination brought no clue as to cause of her problem and I withdrew some blood from a vein for laboratory examination, with Lyme disease in mind.

"Come to see me in two days for the results and a review," I advised.

Angela was subdued when she arrived back. I have had two more events and they seem to be affecting more of my face, although they only last for a few minutes. I was examining her face again when she gave a grunt. Her jaw began to tremor and went into a muscular spasm. I was shocked to see her left thumb and hand were also jerking slightly. The contractions only lasted a few moments. Now I was very worried about the underlying process that was affecting her. Something in the brain was disturbing the nerve pathways. A brain-bleed and minor stroke was a possibility, with more sinister space-occupying lesions in the brain to be considered.

"I think we need to get a hospital opinion for you. I shall fix one", as I lifted the telephone to contact a physician.

"I suppose it will take a few weeks," she suggested.

"No. I want you seen right away."

"I need to get back to work;" she said firmly, I have patients to see."

Her commitment to work was taking priority over her personal health This consideration for others I would to see repeatedly over following weeks. Brushing aside her protests, I sent her off to the local hospital where she was seen by the admitting junior house physician. He examined Angela, then telephoned to say that a skull x-ray and routine tests had been negative and he was sending her home.

Alarmed at this prospect, I intervened, the consultant physician agreed to order a CT (computerised tomography) scan of the brain. Specialised radiographic and ultrasound examinations of the body, especially the brain, were still in their infancy, results were difficult to interpret and only the major city hospital's had the equipment and reporting resources. My intervention speeded the investigative process and the scan was reported as clear a few days later.

Rejoicing, Angela insisted on a return to work. She listened pensively to my forebodings that she might still have some serious pathology, but rightly pointed out that it could prove to be a local, nerve disturbance. In admirable control of her emotions, whatever her inner doubts, and assuring me that colleagues were supportive, she went back to her work routine. I was left with a feeling that she had a more serious disorder than the patients she was treating in the rehabilitation unit.

A week later, Angela's house neighbour phoned to say that she had fallen on the doorstep and had been writhing uncontrollably for some minutes. My emergency-call to her home found her shaken, worried and sleepy. She had suffered a seizure!

"My vision blurred and my hand started to shake and it went right up my arm." she muttered. Something in her brain was causing a focus of abnormal electrical activity and energising the nerves to the arm.

"Was this epilepsy?" she then asked, and I dreaded the further questions her professional training would prompt. Why and what is causing it? I could not prevaricate.

"There is a trigger in your brain, perhaps a small blood clot or a narrowed blood vessel." I hesitated to voice my worry that there might be something even more sinister causing the brain activity. A brain tumour now loomed large as a diagnosis. At her age however, there was a good chance that this might be a benign lesion, removable by surgery or radio-therapy.

"We need to have you admitted for further investigation." She considered this for a moment, then typically said,

"I will go in after work."

"No, now," I said peremptorily, "the ambulance is on its way." She was still protesting her need to return to her patients, when the paramedic team arrived to hasten her transfer to a ward in the Borders Hospital.

Later in the week, after my ward-round in the geriatric unit, I slipped in to see her in the medical ward.

"I have to go Edinburgh for further investigations," she informed me. Another CT scan has been reported and the physician thinks it is a TIA (a transient ischaemic attack)-which usually meant a blood-vessel disturbance or bleed in the brain, Although serious and a rude psychological shock for a young person in apparently good health, this was manageable. She was philosophical about her condition and optimistic. An attitude she would maintain in the months ahead.

"I can get back to work next week." She considered. Her first thoughts as usual were for her patients and colleagues.

"Well, there will have to be a few more investigations to confirm the cause," I counselled.

"As an outpatient," she said, "What about the seizures? I am to have tablets to settle them. I will not be able to drive for some months, but I shall be able to get round my patient's on foot, or by bus," she asserted, with thoughts still on work. Considerate of others as always, she added, "I do not want my colleagues to be over-burdened."

On arrival home, my wife advised that there was an urgent call to Mrs. Pose, who had apparently had a fall. On arrival at her house, I had to fight my way through an over-excited crowd of relatives to reach her prostrated body. It completely blocked one side of the bedroom. She had fallen betwixt bed and window wall and was jammed between.

"What happened?" I asked a small, shrivelled man who was sitting haplessly on the bed, distancing himself from the affray.

"I'm Willie" To my surprise, he was the gargantuan Addie's husband. "She started shaking in bed, and then fell on the floor and was shaking all over. I could not stop her."

Clearing the crowd from the room, I kneeled above Addie who was for once silent. Her face was ashen and blood was coming from her tongue, which she had bitten. She was wheezing for breath. In response to my questions, she slurred an unrecognisable reply and her face drooped to one side with saliva drooling from her lips. With dead-weight draped across the floor and massive chest, abdomen and grossly swollen limbs spread-eagled and crammed against the wall, she looked like a felled elephant in final demise.

Out of habit, I felt for a wrist pulse, but could feel nothing through many inches of fat. The sleeve of my blood-pressure measure was not wide enough to embrace her massive upper arm and defied further check of her clinical status. A brain-stroke was a likely diagnosis, but the list of differential diagnoses encompassed epilepsy and other brain lesions. She needed hospitalisation, but how this would be accomplished was a logistic challenge. I phoned the ambulance service,

"I think you will need help from the fire-service," when thinking of their lifting devices. This got a facetious response.

"You will need a reinforced, large size bed," I advised the admitting house physician. Driving home, I contemplated on how chance could bring two similar presentations to two dissimilar people within a few hours.

Next morning, the surgery staff was gossiping about Addie's transfer to hospital, an account of which had made the Border Herald newspaper. Ignoring my warning instruction, a conventional ambulance had turned up with two tiny paramedics. They had promptly sent for reinforcements who quickly admitted defeat. The fire-brigade had come to the rescue. Addie was transferred through the bed-room window, after the frame was removed from the wall. She had apparently recovered her voice during this procedure had complained bitterly about being mishandled.

Angela was discharged from hospital the same day. I met her later in the week in the rehabilitation ward. She was attending to Mrs. Pose who had suffered a small bleed in the brain and a mild stroke, with loss of power in one arm. The grossly obese woman had been put on a reducing diet by ward staff and was whining on about being starved. True to form, she refused to do the physical convalescent exercises that Angela encouraged her to do, to regain power in the affected arm. She sat immobile and resentful, overflowing her chair, complaining of perceived minor injustices in her care. Angela, disregarding her own health problems, patiently tolerated her complaints, then continued her cheerful, caring round of patients,

Two days later a telephone call from the hospital advised that an urgent appointment was being arranged for Angela. A neurologist had seen the CT reports and there was concern about the nature of the lesion seen in the brain. CT was still a new and rationed procedure with only a few machines available at specialised regional hospitals and this was an anxiety-provoking development.

"It's a precautionary measure," I tried to reassure Angela as she prepared to travel to Edinburgh for the investigation, but I dreaded that a more sinister diagnosis was inevitable.

Shortly after, she had a full blown grand mal, epileptic seizure while at work and was readmitted to the Borders hospital. She had been unconscious with clonic seizures of her limbs. A frightening sight for on-lookers, this attack leaves the victim dazed, stuporous and psychologically challenged. On a whim, I slipped into Angela's room after visiting my geriatric patients and found the room filled with flowers from her patients and colleagues-a measure of her popularity. She was understandably upset and concerned. I could say little to reassure her, although still hoping that there might still be a happy therapeutic outcome.

As we chatted, a senior doctor who was unknown to me, swept into the room. A small ward with four occupied beds separated only by adjustable curtains. He approached Angela and pulled the surrounding bed curtain, which provided an illusion of privacy, but no sound- proofing, Neighbouring patients could hear the ensuing conversation. I could see that Angela, who prized her privacy, was unhappy with this arrangement. He stood beside her for a moment looking at his notes, then without preamble announced,

"I am "Professor........., head of neurology. I have had a look at your X ray images." Without further fore-warning or finesse he went on, "You have a malignant tumour which is incurable and you have perhaps eight months without treatment. My team may offer operation. If it is 60% successful, radio-therapy, or chemotherapy may be possible. You will have to decide. Let us know." With these condemnatory, uncaring words and without a word of compassion or commiseration, he readjusted the curtains and strode off.

His abrupt conduct and unexpected revelation in such a public manner felt like a personal kick in the stomach. I was appalled at this callous mode of communication, which lacked empathy, understanding and fellow-feeling and deeply ashamed that a doctor could behave in such a manner. He had brusquely and brutally informed Angela of the imminent, premature end to her life.

Deeply shocked and saddened, I turned to Angela, who, if stunned by this dreadful news, rallied quicker than I to what effectively was a death-sentence. She had moved abruptly from independence as a fit, young woman with many potential years ahead of her, to a projected life-span of a few months. I struggled for words of consolation. She gallantly came to my rescue.

"What does an operation entail?" I hastily gathered my thoughts, hid my emotions and explained the condition and potential management, trying desperately to alleviate the impact of this dreadful prognosis.

Invasive tumours are often found in the front of the brain and arise from the star-shaped cells which make up the supportive tissue. They are usually highly malignant (cancerous), because the cells reproduce quickly and are supported by a large network of blood vessels. Because the tumour can grow rapidly, the most common symptoms are usually caused by increased pressure in the brain and can include headache, nausea, vomiting, and drowsiness. Depending on location, patients can develop symptoms such as weakness on one side of the body, memory and speech difficulties, and visual changes.

Characteristically, Angela rallied with courage, determination and an aplomb I could not share.

"I shall have the operation", she determined, "I will think positively and commit to getting better." Whatever the inner doubts, her attitude never changed over ensuing, physically-demanding and psychologically challenging months of invasive treatment. Her optimistic, cheerful demeanour embraced relatives, colleagues and health professionals and was steadfast. It was rare for me to meet such personal courage, thoughtfulness and care for others which Angela displayed.

I was furious at the crass, unprofessional behaviour shown by a senior professional colleague in revealing the diagnosis and probable outcome. Neurologists, engrossed in their craft and concentrating on brain structure, can perform poorly in patient rapport, but his total lack of consideration and disinterest for a patient's feelings was remarkable. I was tempted to report his conduct to the General Medical Council but, "whistle-blowing" was not a feature of professional practice in the seventies.

I could only try to lessen the effect of his fatal words on my patient. This was a worst case scenario for Angela, thrust on her without preparation, or counselling. The chances had been in favour of a simple blood-vessel irregularity, or a tumour which could be easily removed, or slow growing and amenable to therapy. Angela had however a vicious, aggressive, fast-growing brain-growth, a malignant cancer destroying brain-tissue and injuring nerves, which would ultimately rob her of faculties and independence.

The prospect was soul-destroying. Working as she did with victims of brain disease, she was fully aware of what lay ahead. A terminal-event was inevitable and I could only hope to ease her suffering. She fixed her sights however on a happy outcome and showed indomitable courage and fortitude, as the disease eroded her physical and mental attributes.

In the interim, Adipose Addie, as I thought of her, regained full use of hand and arm, returned home and became a regular house-call requestor, to plague me on home-visits. She would sit bemoaning her lot, resisting attempts to minimise her bulk and reduce personal health risk. She misused the health and social services and lived as a burden on society; while Angela's productive life was ebbing away.

Valiantly and dispassionately Angela discussed potential therapy. The prognosis, even with treatment, was poor. I wondered if her brave decision to have an operation to remove some of the growth had merely committed her to months of therapeutic side effects, without a good ending. Radio and chemotherapy techniques for treating brain tumours were being developed, but treatment programmes were crude. Therapy destroyed healthy as well as cancer cells and invariably caused nausea, vomiting and fatigue.

“There are risks in surgery,” I had to advise her. “You may be left paralysed, for the tumour is close to vital centres, which will make the surgeon’s job difficult.”

“No. I am having surgery. It will be successful,” she said defiantly on my next ward visit. “The surgeon is coming to see me in a few minutes. If you can wait, we can see him together."

A brisk, fresh-faced, young man soon arrived and perched on the end of her bed. He introduced himself to us boisterously.

“I shall be doing your surgery. I have had a good look at the x-rays and I think we can do a good job here. Now what can I tell you about it?” His easy, charming, manner established a good relationship with Angela in a few minutes. I could only marvel at the difference in approaches demonstrated by two different professionals. The contrast between neurologist and surgeon could not have been more marked. She trustingly transferred to his care in the city hospital. The operation followed promptly with a good outcome.

“The surgeon was able to remove 70% of the tumour without damage to other nerves. I am feeling fine,” she greeted me with a smile, when I visited after her discharge home. “The power in my left hand and arm has returned.” She was again planning to get back to work. I wished I could share her optimism. The operation had bought her time and the opportunity to have radio- therapy which would start shortly. A month later, she came to the surgery for a certificate.

“The seizures have stopped. I am walking short distances and have been back in a kayak again. It was great to be on the water.” I was pleased with her ebullience, and her obvious enjoyment of life. “I am doing yoga, getting physiotherapy to strengthen my hand and find mindfulness helpful, I am planning a big celebration on my next birthday for all those who have helped me.”

I wondered if she would live to see it, but was heartened by her positive attitude, the opposite to Addie’s permanent negativism and refusal to contemplate any means to aid weight-loss and healthier life-style. A few weeks later, when well into the radiotherapy programme, Angela again came to see me.

“Do you like my new hair-style?” she questioned.

“Looks pretty good to me”, I said guardedly. She was now a red-head.

“It’s a wig. I could have had any colour but I thought this was a change.” Hair loss is a devastating challenge to most women, but typically, once again she made light of the impairment.

On completion of the course, her new hair grew in white, a change she accepted with usual good humour.

“Premature ageing. I’ll soon be getting my free bus pass.”

Always a good-looking woman, the white-locks gave her added elegance and as a snappy dresser, few noticed the disability of her left hand and arm which had once again become paralysed. She masked the disability under a scarf, made light of the palsy and continued to maintain her independence, despite intense fatigue associated with radioactive treatment. The blunderbuss therapy was destroying normal blood cells and she became anaemic. In her case I knew that the cancer cells had been very resistant to therapy.

“The oncologist says the tumour has shrunk.” she announced later and I was pleased for her, but feared this was merely a temporary respite.” I am going to have chemotherapy. I wasn’t too sick with the radiotherapy”, as she once again minimised the ill-effects of tumour and treatment.” Then I will get back to work!”.

In ensuing months Angela travelled monthly to the city for debilitating drug treatment which was largely experimental. Doses were tailored to the amount of punishment the body could take and the upset to blood cells. Angela stoically coped with fatigue, nausea and weight-gain which accompanied the treatment. She was swamped with letters and cards from well-wishers and adamantly determined to respond to them herself, despite fatigue that often left her chair-bound.

Six months went by and a call came to visit the family home. Her parents had taken over care when the left leg had become weak and her balance impaired. She was now largely dependent on a wheel-chair to get about.

"Lost my driving license, but I am a whiz kid in a wheel chair," she joked. Her mind was still firmly fixed on cure, as she endured the onslaught of physiotherapists, seizure-control nurses, social workers and well-meaning visitors, with enduring good humour and tolerance. Despite tiredness and increasing disability which she disregarded, she was writing learned articles for professional journals and using her own experiences to suggest practical means of dealing with the consequences of brain tumour. A determination to recover and return to productive work never faltered. To her surprise, professional commitment was recognised by a, 'Best Professional Carer Award' from the NHS. and a commendation for Outstanding Professional Achievement from her professional Association.

"Just doing my job. Didn't merit it" she observed dismissively.

In a few short months however, she had lost her hair, driving licence, job, home and independence. She still showed remarkable spirit, determination and endurance. Physical challenges were there to be overcome. False hopes abounded, with some transient return of limb power or sensation. Clinically I saw an inexorable personal decline. She never gave up hope of a happy outcome, abetted by a mother determined to optimise Angela's days on earth. Relations, friends and colleagues rallied to her aid in testimony to her popularity. The care and attention she had bestowed upon them, they were pleased to return.

Although determined to seek cure, she was philosophical about life.

"I do not fear death, but I am concerned about suffering." Words that would haunt me over the next few months, as the effects of treatment had a devastating effect upon her. The tumour once again began to advance. Despite the aid of a small army of health carers, and therapists, the disease marched on. She suffered increasing infirmity, loss of intimate personal functions and total loss of independence but, never failed to bolster the feelings of those close to her and praise all involved in her health care.

Addie in the meanwhile had become a permanent resident in the local care home and as a resident remained one of my patients. She had regained the full use of all her limbs, but had taken to an outsize, reinforced wheel-chair, heaved around by staff. Immobile, her legs were elephantine and she needed extra staff and lifting-devices to get in and out of bed – a major logistic exercise. She circumvented efforts to reduce her weight, by inveigling husband and visitors to bring in dietary treats. She scolded staff, derided relatives and complained incessantly about her plight and nursing and medical care. A burden on the state and drain on scarce resources, I found her obnoxious and our consultations unpleasant and unproductive.

"I need stronger water pills," she would accost me. "You need to give me stronger pain-killers for my knees." The demands were constant, totally self centred and her condition largely self-inflicted. I often compared her behaviour to the selfless, uncomplaining conduct of the terminally-ill Angela,

She still worked doggedly at exercises to strengthen affected limbs and hoped for ultimate tumour eradication. There were false dawns, when x-rays indicated some tumour regression to hearten patient and carers, but these proved cruelly misleading. The advance of the cancer was relentless, bringing further loss of remaining physical faculties.

The family adapted to the demands of the disease and Angela's needs, converting a room into a virtual ward, with hospital bed and accoutrements. Lifting devices, mobility aids and nursing paraphernalia confirmed the extent of her invalidity. She slept a lot and I was grateful that she remained free of headaches and epileptic fits. Losing awareness of time, she turned night into day and required round-the-clock care. Mother - now the prime carer - and daughter showed exemplary courage in dealing with ever-increasing incapacity. They both remained optimistic, positive thinking and determined to give their all, in combating the advance of a devastating disease. Their endeavours did not contemplate defeat.

Angela, tried to reduce demand on parents, carers and the NHS and deflected my questions about her status and comfort by quizzing me about my own family. She was adamant that I only visit when she was in dire need and unstintingly praised carers for their attention.

"You have many more deserving patients than me," she would allege and I would leave her once again, marvelling at her attitude and comparing it with the unappreciated work-load generated by the ever demanding Adipose Addie, who relentlessly castigated all who cared for her.

The care home manager would apologise when requesting a visit.

"It's Addie again," she would inform. "She insists she needs the attention of a doctor and will not be put off." I would grudgingly attend, to find Addie the centre of attention and whinging about some minor discomfort.

Angela, became almost bed-bound and doubled in weight due to steroid treatment and immobility. She had to suffer the final indignity of double incontinence, the insertion of a permanent in-dwelling catheter and reliance on nurses and mother for intimate personal care. Feeding became difficult, as swallowing was impaired. As balance was lost, her dependence upon others was absolute. She had gone from staunch, individual, personal independence to total dependence on others in a few short months. The personal adaptations forced by unrelenting adversity would have frustrated, infuriated and depressed most people. She managed these devastating life changes with equanimity. When quizzed about increasing impairments she would invariably reply,

"I am fine doctor. We can manage. How are you?"

Mother, totally dedicated to her daughter's care, would respond in the same vein, although she herself was losing weight and becoming care-worn. I worried that I would soon have two patients to manage as a nervous-breakdown seemed imminent in mum, if not daughter. This became more likely as the tumour began to affect Angela's thinking. She developed fixed ideas and circular-thinking which locked her thoughts in to simple repetitive actions. She would forget that she had just been fed or dressed and insist that the process be repeated – stressing carers. Her night and day demands were unremitting, as awareness of time was lost.

When lucid, she still tried to minimise the impact of her illness on others, struggling to use failing limbs and functions to aid carers and concerned about the pressures her debility placed on the family.

"What about hospital respite care?" I suggested.

"No" intervened Mum and I reluctantly acquiesced, as this would have entailed short-term transfer to a geriatric care ward, quite inappropriate for a young adult. I was relieved at this response, but wondered how long the family could maintain home care.

Chemotherapy with its ravaging side-effects was completed. The oncologist tactfully inferred that the end was nigh, but Angela and Mum would not accept this possibility. Angela may have been deluded and a decline in intellect may have been responsible for her euphoric belief that all might end well, Mum however remained steadfast in her belief of ultimate cure. She refused to consider her daughter's true predicament. I worried that when the inevitable end came, brutal reality for her would be like falling off a psychological cliff and threaten clinical disaster.

A stream of professional carers now attended by day, with mother coping valiantly at night when there were no NHS resources. The epileptic fits returned with a vengeance. Increased medications made Angela somnambulant. In fifteen desperate months, the tumour had changed her from a lissom, eight stone athlete to a corpulent eighteen stone, total invalid. I wondered at the value of the long therapeutic, debilitating trail. Increased longevity had come at high personal price.

After a grand mal seizure, when she fell to the floor, it required a team effort to return her to bed. Further falls and probable hip fractures were certain. Overcoming mum's reluctance, I decreed.

"It is time for hospice care." and arranged respite admission in the local unit. This finally brought mother's realisation that she would lose her daughter. The reaction suggested I would lose one patient and pick up another. Angela realised the significance of this institutional admission, but refused to acknowledge a short term future and optimistically continued plans for the year ahead.

She charmed the hospice staff with her concern for them, continued in lucid moments to advise them on physiotherapy tips on handling patients and had favoured patient status.

"I am a diva here." She assured me, praising the staff lavishly. A few days later she entered a coma which lasted for ten days before she slipped away.

Several hundred people attended her funeral and colleagues lauded her achievements and were saddened at her passing. I could only marvel at her great fortitude and courage in the face of crippling adversity and the devotion of a mother, who had provided unstinting support and care to the end.

Addie however continued to live on as a permanent resident of the care home in unappreciated receipt of scarce health service resources. She alienated husband, family and professional staff and was an entrenched "heart-sink "patient who long plagued me and practice staff. Institutionalised, bereft of visitors and shunned by staff, she ultimately lived, isolated in a world of her own making. Selfish, self-centred and a drain on society, I adversely contrasted her useless existence, with the giving, selfless, behaviour of Angela.

Her early death left many grieving at the premature end to a productive life and the loss of a caring friend. In many years in practice, I rarely met such contrasting personalities.

Master or Servant?

Passing years brought a technological revolution which had a dramatic effect on doctor, patient and the medical consultation. In a decade, we were swept from laborious hand- written and typewriter recorded notes into the digital age of computer word processing. A sucker for innovation, I acquired one of the first home market machines, a revolutionary Sinclair ZX81 introduced in 1981, Price: £65. Half a million were sold in the first 12 months. It weighed 12 ounces had 64 K of memory and a ROM BASIC operating system which required new linguistic skills in the operator, but it had potential medical practice use.

This began a long love/hate relationship bringing opportunity and frustration, elation and heart-break, anger and achievement. Neither textbook, nor on-line support was available. Trial and error was the order of the day. The emphasis was on binary numbers - an innovative concept for the lay-man - and a new language. It had to be mastered before gaining computer competence. Determined to assimilate the art and use the it professionally, I attended educational evening classes. Teachers assiduously revealed how ones and zeroes could wizard their way through complex mathematics to solutions, which previously would have taken a half day of conventional calculation to achieve.

Impressed by the technical potential and encouraged to write simple programmes. I failed this first hurdle as did many colleagues. The simplest instruction,

"If one equals ... then zero equals ... ?" required complicated data input. Instructions had to be loaded on to magnetic tape, transferred to the machine, absorbed and regurgitated in meaningful script. For every correct response, others were invariably produced as hieroglyphics. Interaction was tediously time-consuming. In a short time, my partners became disenchanted. The embryonic computer was returned to its packing case and stored in the attic, until passing years made it a valuable antique.

Shortly after its rejection, the first word processors arrived on the scene, with a wealth of associated jargon. The viewing screen was tiny, but they accepted terse, typed commands like "Go Tos" and "Remove". Memory stores consisted of about 40 kilobytes and opening programmes required a retentive memory for numbers, slashes and alphabet items. A single error and access was denied. In the absence of installed dictionaries and spell checks, grammatical and spelling mistakes predominated in documents. Linking output to first generation embryonic printers was problematic, with print quality little threat to traditional typewriters.

Printers had a voracious thirst for ink, supplied in reservoirs wont to leak. Re-supply required juggling of syringes and bottles. Refill left indelible stains on fingers, computers and desks from inevitable spills. Ink-transport often blocked and clearance was dependent upon delicate manoeuvres with a screw-driver, which tried patience. Their arrival heralded the death knell for the Imperial type-writer and threatened the demise of the typist, both previously dominant in every surgery and clinic. The administrative technological (IT) revolution was just beginning. Computers would eventually threaten conventional spelling capabilities, with Americanised dictionaries and lexicons thrusting aberrant spelling on English users.

Amstrad's introduction of Locoscript, with mini-menus appearing out of the blue, was a major advance in technology. One-touch key bar operations became possible, if one could remember what hot-key symbols represented and in what sequence" control, alt and function" keys were used. Long documents became possible and were stored on diskettes which had to be formatted laboriously before use. Menus were no longer the sole domain of the chef and they spawned hidden submenu offspring, to tempt, tease and frustrate the operator.

Voice recognition software arrived and long hours were wasted educating the machine to recognise spoken words. Launched ahead of their time, they brilliantly recognised speech and would regurgitate words verbatim in quantity, but dubious quality. My head cold and slurred words would send the unit into a frenzy of word misrecognition and flood the document with almost unintelligible script. Their best efforts required many document corrections. They did not take kindly to the many medical terms common to my reports. After a tedious trial, the soft-ware was discarded and touch-typist skills developed.

New words entered my vocabulary. "Computer crash, glitch, break-down and failure" came to replace blame attributed to human administrative incompetence and human weakness. Traditional words took on greater significance with "start, save, save as, file and folder" having nuances of their own. The logic of some often defeated me. What inspired programmer determined that one had to enter "start" to route to "exit, end, close?" Frustrated without this knowledge and faced with a stalled machine, I trashed programmes by turning off the power supply.

Hard and soft-ware, internal and external drives were a minefield for the novice and I soon realised that self-declared "experts" in the field had limited expertise and experimentation, their operative default mode. Computer literate patients were often greeted with requests for digital information before I embarked on their medical problems. Several times they saved me from computer oblivion when the monster was intent on self- destruction.

The unobtrusive mouse crept into the computer scene with its click commands bringing emancipation from the demands of the keyboard. Initially a simple switch with a long-tailed wire connection, it developed a life of its own, with rollers, buttons and gadgets to further complicate data-entry and recall, and further overload personal memory. The nuisance of entangling wire-leads departed, when the appliance was liberated with the arrival of Wi-Fi connection. The dongle and toggle had come to stay.

Finally freed from restraints of pen and paper I could now direct hundreds of words of inspiration into the machine. Swept away by creative frenzy, all too often a miss-key, or electronic foible would see irreplaceable words of talent disappear permanently from the screen. Frenzied search through inventories, files and folders would follow, but rarely could these hallowed thoughts and words be retrieved.

The computer was establishing the dominance of machine over man in the surgery and intervening between doctor and patient with the former's eye contact more often with the impersonal machine than with the patient. Many times the lesson to "save in-put regularly" was forgotten. The ensuing, agonising, time-consuming trawl of the machine's inner workings invariably confirmed that crucial content was gone for ever.

Increasing hardware memory stores competed with and finally excelled my memory capacity and bulky patient files came to be stored on diskettes, disks, memory cards/sticks/pens and hard drives. Kilobytes were replaced by megabytes then gigabytes and terabytes with hundreds, thousands and finally millions of bits of data stored for posterity. Access required scrupulous recall of individual passwords and data entry. Human fallibility determined there was duplication and miss-entry, ensuring future dubiety when searching for retrievable input. Incompatibility between machines, add-ons and soft-ware added to the need for good personal memory recall. Inevitable amnesic moments forced recourse to reminders on hard copy and reliance paradoxically on paper and pen. Long-heralded paperless administration was slow to materialise.

A few weeks separation from computer-input often brought the embarrassment of denied electronic access, through shortcomings in personal memory, over- reliance on circuitry and software foibles. Further psychological trauma was sustained with any failure to record details of menu access, electronic shortcuts and passwords. A marvel of ingenuity and a passport to a new world of innovation, the computer was proving a stress-inducing, anxiety-provoking, recalcitrant work-horse in the surgery.

The innards of the magic machine were acquiring human characteristics. The apparatus could prove disobedient in refusing instructions and over-bearing, when proffering unsolicited and unwanted observations on grammar or procedure. The infernal beast demonstrated an innate ability to display aberrant behaviour and develop its own hidden agenda. It would "go slow", refuse to save, blank/grey out or freeze the screen at a time of maximal psychological upset to myself.

Punctilious, prompt response to commands for hours would suddenly be replaced by profound reluctance to perform any activity, especially the saving or printing of important documents, on completion of a laboriously completed interaction, or at a deadline. Failed commands or screen message that peremptorily state,

"A terminal event has occurred, data will be lost and automatic switch off is in process" created heart-sink moments threatening cardiac arrest, with the realisation that all recent work input is gone and has to be repeated.

The appliance, despite its own petulant behaviour, reacted aggressively to my misdemeanours. It could arbitrarily refuse to read discs or data from other computers, coyly demanding formatting of its choice. Any unexpected power supply interruption had it retreat in prolonged sulk, threatening never to load any programme again. Unwanted mechanical interference would see it die for ever, with unintended exposure to excess heat and cold or fluid a mortal intervention. The dropping of a few spots of spilt coffee on a keyboard brought a frenzy of asterisks, exclamation marks and swear words to the screen showing its displeasure at an incursion into the works. Recovering function proved a tedious costly experience. The machine would repeatedly remind of the unwanted intrusion in later months, with the appearance of a profusion of opaque words, if the home key was engaged.

A new syndrome developed in practice patients bringing behavioural change. Computer aversion crept into daily life becoming ever more prominent and threatening to create a division in society between "computer literate and illiterate". In time this began to separate young from old, husband and wife. Nursery pupils were educated into the alchemy of computer science, whereas senior citizens spurned the black art. Computer phobia began to afflict many. Computer-addiction affected youngsters who eye-balled the computer screen for hours on end. The infernal machinery began to affect the nation's health, with computer-induced headaches, stress, and eye-strain generated by the flickering screen and repetitive stress syndrome affected necks, wrists and joints

Small computers had initially sneaked into businesses and surgery offices, with initiation of simple computer-generated bills and invoices laboriously created for each client appearing in the post. Computer generation of lists brought the potential for mass data storage and bulk mailings and the computer age was launched nation-wide. Government, business and professions saw huge potential for machinery to store patient data.

Padding out dubious personal experience of the demanding machines and exaggerating enthusiasm for new technology, I applied for a Government business grant and purchased a £16,000 computer with less memory than a child's computer toy of today. It took months to programme in data and consistently stalled when confronted with repetitive data input on Chinese individuals named Lee. They all were on the practice list! Its deficiencies did not prevent rollout to NHS Primary Care with system-failures that took decades to eradicate.

Small Amstrad palm-held devices arrived with a fanfare. They proved to be nothing more than inadequate notelets requiring written data input via a plastic stylus on the touch screen - a finger fiddle. A glorified diary ahead of its time, it was the precursor of the Blackberry and iPod and was typically incompatible with other computers.

The evolution of operating systems ultimately brought change, with the arrival of Word Perfect and a renewed struggle to again master the vagaries of new soft-ware. Large support books came with the machine, with content often as difficult to interpret as the software. Then with further evolution on-line versions made them obsolescent.

Computers were initially very large, with detached weighty, unwieldy visual display units the size of cathode ray televisions The first portable ones, with Amstrad to the fore, appeared and the first pseudo lap-top promised mobility. The size of a large portable typewriter with a very heavy battery, it finally offered computing without wired power supply. Books were written directly to screen. Saving contents to flexible floppy discs promised permanent storage and retrieval, but time brought data corruption. The next generation of computers brought in rigid floppy discs with greater storage capacity, but incompatibility with former diskettes. These became obsolescent with obsolescence now the name of the game.

The industry spawned hard and software at a phenomenal rate with the microchip revolution. New computers became out of date within weeks. The next onslaught brought Windows application, Word software and a camera - the digital camera had arrived. New software had to be mastered again and previous knowledge largely discarded. The computer was mated with a large instruction manual and on-line support. This ultimately made the manual an anachronism, to the dismay of all those preferring to read printed information. Memory facility was many times that of its forebears, but a hundred times less than its successors. Amstrad also brought out a neat little word processor the size of a library book dependent on memory discs for storage, the fore runner of the later word book, still 20 years away.

An enduring desktop model once lasted seven or eight years, then the microchip revolution advanced miniaturising hardware and brought undreamed applications. Divorce of hardware tower, key-board, VDU and printer heralded the arrival of the lap-top. Portability depended upon the battery with its thirst for recharging at intervals of initially half an hour. The portable laptop ensured the beast became a permanent companion, going on trains, planes and holidays. Its evolution and the advent of electronic communication introduced a new revolution. Overnight one could contact locations across the world and with Google, accumulated global data transfer was only a few clicks away.

Suddenly, the security of the personal computer disappeared.The operator was exposed to electronic aggression and a flood of new nomenclature. "Hackers, skimmers, phishers, scams" invaded the scene. Electronic surveillance and data theft became a constant threat to privacy and safety. "Worms, bugs and viruses" were no longer the domain of the doctor and horticulturalist, but were an everyday concern for every computer user. They could be and were introduced into state-of-the-art nuclear programmes to derail construction of nuclear war-heads, by nations in political conflict. Belatedly there came forced recognition of unhealthy dependence upon the ubiquitous computer.

Loss of access, disappearance of data, corruption of files, stolen personal information and identity brought realisation of an overdependence upon a machine once a servant and now the master. The wondrous access to data and people across the world was compromised by international rogues and charlatans. Continued enthralment with the IT revolution could not be denied however as ever more technological wonders were unveiled.

E-mails undermined the GPO institution and digitalisation of photography threatened demise of the high street photographer. The computer could in seconds enhance any photograph and send it round the world, or store it and its fellows in albums on distant servers and with cloud technology possibly somewhere in outer space. The IT effect on hospital investigation and administration was profound and suddenly patients and family doctors had to come to terms with computerised tomography(CT) and magnetic resonance image (MRI) screening of every part of the anatomy.

Electronic mailing flooded surgery in-boxes with a plethora of unwanted mail and "face book, linked in, and twitter" encouraged intimacy with other health professionals and distant individuals in cosy, potentially unsavoury, interaction. Broad-band communication brought downloading of sound and vision of television and film onto the personal screen and challenged the need for a daily newspaper. I could e-mail gps. in branch surgeries for information quicker than I could telephone them. The surgery consultation lost some of its intimacy and isolation.

The advent of "Kindle" threatened conventional books and libraries and touch-pads pointed the route forward. The "paperless medical practice was a Government objective and with it came mass input of patient records with more distant history destined for microfiche storage and lost to easy access. No longer could I explore a patient's envelope-held record and plumb their history back to child-birth, a resource only appreciated after it was lost.

The appearance of the "tablet" suggests that, future miniaturisation and an alternative power source will ensure that mini-computers of massive functional capacity will be carried in every pocket. They will universally replace pen, and telephone, providing global communication at the touch of a button. There seems no end to technological innovation and advancement. Digitalised technology brought change to general medical practice and threatened the family doctor's mastery of the surgery. It is difficult to perceive life without this remarkable invention, but permanently robbed of power input, the machinery would be mere junk, with global financial and administrative and medical melt-down - a scenario best left unexplored.

The former roomful of computer machinery has been reduced to the size of an A4 notepad with memory thousands of times that of its early predecessors, Unfortunately it has retained the same innate tendencies to crash, cause mayhem and speed into obsolescence. Within three decades the computer revolution has changed human behaviour with no end in sight to its ultimate advancement. It has brought many wonders, much anguish, frustration and agony, As a constant companion it is here to stay. Its demise might topple Governments, disintegrate economies and bring profound personal bereavement. The servant has undoubtedly become the master and is here to stay! In retrospect disposable syringes and treatment packs, the mobile telephone and computer were the forces that inspired change, for better or worse, in primary medical care in my time as a family doctor.

Pastures New

In the sixties, family doctor salaries were poor - less than £1,500 per annum at a time when a small semi-detached bungalow cost £7000. Mortgage repayments ate into income and we had perforce to be frugal. I converted a rubble-strewn walled garden at the rear of the surgery into a vegetable garden and in time took over the vacant office plot next door for a fruit-growing area. Waiting "on-call" in the evenings, I would labour with pick-axe and spade to prepare the hard-trodden, neglected ground for planting.

There was an Italian restaurant next door to the surgery and Fredo the owner was one of my patients. He had osteo-arthritis affecting one knee. This would flare-up, when he had to stand for long periods, an occupational hazard as he slaved for long hours in the kitchen. Fredo had been a prisoner-of-war who had worked in the farmlands of Fife and married a local girl. Always working under pressure, he would slip Bette a prescription request for an anti-inflammatory preparation. This was usually written on a bar-paper slip or, when hard-pressed, a beer mat. Although he had mastered English speech, his vocabulary was limited and flowery. His spelling tested Bette's powers of interpretation. A 'glooey oyntminte,' was one of his favourites. This was ultimately dispensed as a tarry, foul-smelling paste once given to him by my predecessor, in which he put much faith. I was dubious of its therapeutic properties. However, it seemed a beneficial placebo, without side-effects associated with anti-arthritic drugs and I acceded to his requests

"A luffly efening," he would observe, from a sheltered alcove in his garden in a few moments of respite while awaiting customers. We would share a few pleasantries before he slipped back to his kitchen. Occasionally, while I was delving in the garden, a disembodied voice would come from across the boundary wall,

"A lite bite Doctore," and a laden tray of food would be pushed over the high garden wall for my consumption. Complete with napkin and glass of wine, I would contentedly scoff the lot sitting among the plants and bless a grateful patient.

With large tins strung around necks, our small children would pick the ripe raspberries in the autumn and despite woeful cries of,

"I don't like the worms," and "I'm frightened of spiders," helped crop potatoes and carrots. The harvest helped feed the growing family.

Surgery consultations were key elements in my working week. In days before practice nurses and specialised GP. Clinics for obstetrics, diabetes, hypertension and asthma, their content varied remarkably. Physical examinations, prescriptions and injections were interspersed with demands for sickness notes, vaccinations, suturing, boil lancing, ear-syringing and even ear-piercing. The latter was a little money earner as one of the few occasions we could charge for the service, with half a crown changing hands when a young woman insisted on keeping up with fashion. There was invariably variety and one never knew what presentation might appear

Consultations could be tedious but never boring and sometimes there would be strange runs when consecutives patients would present similar maladies or conditions. One after the other individuals would troop in with heart conditions, asthma or depression. On one particular morning it was minor injuries – self-inflicted injury.

Averil was the first. A nineteen year old from a very disturbed family background, she offered her forearms for examination. This was not her first surgery call. Product of a failed marriage and subjected to family abuse, she was a very unhappy teenager. In the absence of any other NHS support, I had spent time on counselling. Her inner conflicts had been partly resolved and she had found a boy-friend and gone off happily with him.

Now she was back presenting superficial, but long lacerations in her arm where. The boy had walked out on her and once again, unable to handle the psychological trauma, she had attacked herself physically. Averil responded to adversity by self-harming. As I bandaged the wounds, I listened to her story and tried once again to give her more appropriate means of dealing with her mind disturbance.

Next person through the door was Harry who worked in the local betting shop and was better at calculating the odds than wielding tools. He had responded to his wife's nagging about a sticking cupboard door by attacking it with a wood chisel which slipped. The sharp blade had carved a lengthy gouge out of his thigh, which I had to stitch. He departed with a limp to be replaced by Nessie fresh from her house-work .A bar-maid, she was more effective at pulling pints than painting and had managed to spill a bottle of paint stripper over her hands when house decorating. The burnt, blistered skin was testimony to the efficacy of the liquid as a solvent and I chastised heras I attended to the wounds.

"You will have to take more care and precautions to avoid injury. It is only a few months since you fell off a ladder cleaning your windows and cracked your skull".

Next in was Alex, the minister from the nearby church, who had been standing on a pew to change a light bulb and had fallen off. He now presented woefully with a badly swollen ankle. It was not broken but badly sprained - divine intervention perhaps. Severely overworked and stressed, I had recently advised him to take time off, a suggestion he ignored. Now I ordered,

"You will have to take time off. No weigh-bearing for a week".

This string of events had me contemplate how much work, self-inflicted injury added to my work-load. Then it slipped into mind that I was not exempt from criticism in this respect. Unprofessional labour and self-inflicted injury had become concomitant with my "on-call" and spare time. "On call" dominated hours away from the surgery. In the absence of casualty units and "walk-in" centres the GP.at home, or in surgery, was the emergency resource of first recourse, Out-patient departments turned away casual callers and patients identified the GP as provider for first aid and urgent care. We sutured, bandaged, splinted fractures and dealt with home and road accidents in this role. "On call" was onerous but, in between incidents there was much spare time interrupted only by demands of the telephone, an opportunity for house-bound and building tasks.

Home was too small for growing needs, but funds would not permit removal to a larger place, or the hire of tradesmen for conversion projects. Harview our house in Riverside had appeared a good buy, to suit the impoverished pocket. Long vacant, it came with a legacy of neglect and a maintenance deficit requiring years of DIY attention. Over the next decade, I spent as much time as a labourer and builder as I did doctoring. I would rush home from the surgery, don overalls and start making cement for bricklaying. The prime of our lives went on the building. Now a monument to constructive indiscretions, it came close to being our cenotaph.

Unprofessional Labours

Student vacation jobs as builder's labourer had provided limited expertise to use a spirit level, lay foundations and double-courses of bricks, build on rooms and extend the house. Consultations with tradesmen patients proved invaluable opportunities to milk information on laying drains, running electrics and building roofs.

"How do you recess hinges on a door", I would ask Jim the carpenter when he consulted with his bad back or, "What is the polarity on a double electric switch?" of Ned the electrician, who had a regularly recurring dermatitis needing skin prescriptions. I hated making up his emoluments which were messy, greasy concoctions, but his advice compensated for the task and brightened our environment. "How much liquid-soap emulsifier do you add to building cement? How deep should foundations be? "greeted Willie the bricklayer, when he arrived with an injured thumb.

Consultations often became a two-way educative process. Patients usually reacted benignly to these inquisitions, which often established a lasting rapport, easing future consultations. They were wryly amused at my amateur efforts, took an interest in building endeavours and would humorously enquire when meeting me on my rounds,

"Is the wall/door still standing doctor? How is the plastering going?"

The ubiquitous DIY trend, with its stores and resources, was a philosophy still in the future. Resourcing materials had to be negotiated through merchants accustomed to dealing with established tradesmen and not construction-ignorant family doctors. The transition from traditional to metric measure was a tedious process and they tolerated my endeavours to convert inches to centimetres.

"Better stick to your scalpel Doc," they would advise.

Concrete and brick-laying were constant activities as we added rooms. Bricks were not pre-packaged and five tons of loose sand and a thousand bricks would be unceremoniously dumped at the house-gates. Their removal required a Herculean effort, as they blocked road- traffic. The whole family was mobilised, with Victoria - the four year old - wheeling three bricks in her toy barrow to the storage pile. All learned to mix cement and lay bricks, activity which might now be interpreted as child exploitation.

I did engage a squad of bricklayers once for the first room extension and ordered insufficient sand for the project. Employed on one of their rare half-day holidays, they quickly ran out of sand for cement. Quarries and sand-merchants were closed and building was grounding to a halt. I remembered that when moving a clothes-pole in the middle of the rear lawn, I had come across a layer of pristine shingle and beneath it, beautiful white sand. The house was built on a raised beach, the bank of a primeval river.

I hastily dug down into the lawn, bared shingle and sand, scooped out material and barrowed it directly to labourers. Cement went immediately to brick layers who completed their task. Ignoring mineral rights, this unexpected resource became a small mine, which provided sand for much later building.

"Hey, oops, wha's tha dooin' there?" would come jovially from Archie the farmer, as he passed up the lane on his tractor. From his perch, he could peer over the garden hedge and was intrigued at the sight of my legs sticking up through a hole in the ground. After digging down for six feet, I began to extract the sand laterally and soon had a gallery running under the garden, with walls restrained by props. Mindful of the "Great POW Escape" of World War Two, when wall-sides collapsed on the excavators, I finally closed the working when reaching the neighbour's boundary. Years later, a gentle, linear subsidence across the lawn is a reminder of these mining days.

By then, I had manually built on three rooms, carport, boiler-house, toilets and workshop. Bungled attempts at joinery in childhood had burgeoned into unexpected expertise in building construction. In retrospect these labours were a physical outlet for the psychological stresses of family doctoring and lightened the burden of long "on call" hours.

Self Inflicted Injury

"Bad backs" were a common patient complaint, now often a result of leisure time activity but in the sixties and seventies often the result of bad work practices. Labourers and coal delivery men hoisted large hundred weight bags on and off their shoulders through the working day. Miners hefted huge pit props into place and farmers wrestled with large animals and heavy machinery. Work-shirkers used the label as an excuse to avoid work, but most patients sought a pain killer and stoically continued at work. Many back injuries however began to occur in unfit, men in non-manual occupations who, short of cash, turned to self-initiated home improvement.

Jimmie was one of them. A wages clerk he had recently moved into a small bungalow. His house proud wife Abby and he started on lengthy renovation and redecorating, until he suffered a fall.. On my house call she greeted me.

"He was fitting a new door bell and I told him to get the ladder, but he insisted he could do it standing on a chair." She said accusingly.

"The chair slipped." he said sheepishly. "I have got really bad pain across my back and down the leg."

"He really can't move without severe pain," Abbey added more sympathetically. On examination, he had disturbed nerve reflexes and boarding of the back muscles which suggested he had injured a vertebral disc. Prolonged back rest was then the treatment.

"Your lack of safety precautions has cost you dear. You will be off work for some time." I observed I left a disconsolate Jimmie contemplating many weeks of work and a cessation of house renovation. As I left the house, I realised that my words had been hypocritical. I had embarked on many of my own self-involved home improvements. Many brought unforeseen threats to my personal health.

The penury of early doctoring years encouraged "Do it yourself," when the expression DIY had yet to be coined. I altered, renovated and created much of our home and its environs. Financial and time constraints usually meant the wrong tool for the job and a frenzied rush to complete work squeezed round conventional surgery hours. Medical training did little to prepare for trials of home maintenance. Orthopaedics had however brought familiarity with chisels, saws, augurs, screw-drivers and braces, all tools of the constructor. Casualty work brought dexterity with knives, clamps and sutures. Obstetrics proved a crash course in manoeuvring tight-fitting objects round corners and artful reconstruction. Laboratory and pharmacy expertise was useful in mixing and thinning paints and varnishes.

The first DIY project was a simple garden shed. The local wood supplier also -the undertaker- took an immediate interest in my wood-work efforts. The assistance was probably driven by an awareness of potential funeral business. All went well initially. The shed was stout of timber and generous in proportions. With roof and sides temporarily assembled, a capricious gust of wind blew the whole structure flat. En route to the ground, it performed a full-length dermabrasion of my upturned face. The stone-impregnated asphalt roof tore its way painfully from scalp to chin, taking with it much of my thinning cranial hair and leaving two blackened eyes.

Patient wags enjoyed my discomfiture,

"Been in a fight then Doc? What's the other man like?" they would comment as they presented for consultation.My appearance was a source of glee for Archie when I turned up at surgery,

"By Goad ye've made a joab o' it. Wir ye kicked by t' bull." The discoloration changed from cyan, to purple, crimson and red, then finally disappeared, but a hint of baldness to come became a permanency. Resultant cranial scars have resisted mellowing by sun and time.

Attention turned to housing needs and a simple internal room-conversion. No hassle here, just a few sheets of hardboard, some nails and hey presto, a room for the newest youngster. One however needs to be ambidextrous to hold and nail very large sheets of boarding to rafters. In extremis, Anne, my long suffering wife, was commandeered to hold the board horizontal while standing on tiptoe on folding steps.

In ensuing contortions, to control wildly-convulsing sheeting defying fixture, an ominous snap heralded internal derangement of vertebrae in her spine. Heroically, she finished the job before retiring to the invalid couch, to face months of lumbago and sciatica. I regularly returned home to find her in fixed immobility on the floor, with tiny tots scrambling across her recumbent figure. Remarkably, an injudicious lunge over a chair two years later brought instant and permanent cure.

Undeterred, I pressed ahead with home insulation and laid fibre glass insulation across the attics. The resultant lung invasion by dust and silica particles gave me a deep-pitched rhonchus, heard several feet away on deep breathing. After living with the oddity for some years, its increasing resonance finally forced a consultation with a chest physician.

"Never heard the like of it before," he remarked and blithely and left me in ownership of unique pathology.

Over-enthusiasm for loft insulation nearly brought untimely demise. Crawling in the minute space between the upper roof-trees at the furthest point of the gable-end, I became inextricably jammed between wood supports and the fibre glass roll being insinuated between body and ceiling. Air was at a premium in this remote, awkward, unlit spot and squashed tightly between roof and rafters, breathing became almost impossible. Dust, thoracic pressure and panic brought impending suffocation and collapse. I felt like a cave-explorer trapped in some hell-hole far from human succour. "Help. Help." I shouted close to asphyxiation. Ann, however, mother of my children was lying on the ground floor in one of her spells of enforced inactivity - not that she could have reached my location anyway. Black-out was imminent, when desperate fingers found a pocketed knife, to hack away dungarees and insulant, allowing air access to lungs and egress for my panic- stricken frame.

Defective valves in the radiator system brought the next item of DIY farce. Ignoring the need to drain the system, we innocently started to change valves, with the water still circulating. The first valve-cover came off and with it came a cascading jet of hot water.

"Quick Anne stop it." She unthinkingly put a finger on the cascade, to remove it just as quickly with a squeal of anguish as it was scalded. Initial dismantling had been deceptively easy. Reassembly however was a nightmare, as fingers cramped and slipped and the water arched to the ceiling, drenching us. Worse was to come with successive valves. Disharmony threatened the end to a happy marriage.

I did not always learn from these dire predicaments. Plumbing problems were common and late one evening, when stripping out an old cupboard from the wall, a chisel went through a copper hot-water pipe. Water spouted from the gash and I thoughtlessly put a thumb over leak to stop the flow. The hole had rough, sharp edges which lacerated the skin and the spout became brick-red as blood joined the stream of hot water. This poured down the inside of my shirt and flowed down legs to flood the floor as I struggled to staunch the escape. With a little more care, I finally stemmed the deluge with bandages and adhesive tape left after rendering first-aid to the wounded appendage.

The next simple task was chimney cleaning. Nothing to it! Drop an iron ball with attached brush down the chimney; shove up a rod brush from below and away with the soot. The project went smoothly. No one fell off the roof and a large fire was lit in the hearth in celebration of success. Alas, a starling had built a substantial nest between the reach of the ball's descent and the ascending rods. Clouds of acrid, noxious fumes filled the room and brought on daughter Jenny's first attack of asthma.

The next trial by fire came when attempting to add a switch to the instrument panel of the car. The cables shorted and flames spread rapidly into the main electric harness and the innards of the vehicle. Eye-brows and remaining hair were badly singed in efforts to halt the conflagration

DIY labours did not all end traumatically, some became wild frolics. In the early days of polystyrene adhesives, we inadvertently became pioneer glue sniffers. A mammoth session of tile-laying in a poorly ventilated room had us both quite euphoric and floating in a blissful seventh heaven, intoxicated with volatile vapour. The advent of super glue enlivened the scene for it stuck fingers to each other and to other objects, but rarely stuck to things we wanted glued. A relatively minor DIY accident led to a split tooth. Attempted repair with super glue, firmly fixed the tooth fragment to the floor after it had fallen there. Ungloved contact with epoxy resins brought contact dermatitis to the hands and an irritating skin itch, which took years to resolve.

The introduction of power tools enlivened DIY activities. Electric shocks were a regular occurrence and threatened cardiac arrhythmia. Conditioned to sudden surges of current we could probably survive exposure to the electric chair.

Tired of my construction mishaps Ann withdrew from the DIY scene and I resorted to "Do it oneself", which inevitably involved the individual movement of heavy loads. Self- reliant, I lifted ridiculously massive weights, until a concrete window lintel brought retribution in the shape of a slipped disc. Enforced bed-rest brought introspective life review and a very brief break from general practice -one week- at a time when disc lesions were routinely treated with six weeks in bed, with traction to the legs. I returned to medical practice less physically able than most of my patients.

The sciatic pain was so intense that any sudden movement brought agony and I conducted consultations while standing. Patients were solicitous and in a reversal of roles helpfully offered their own remedies. "Witch's balm helped my bad back. A guid dram before bed will do the trick. The infra-red got me back on my feet." On one occasion I had to be stretchered home from the consulting room by ambulance, although I returned to work the next day.

A slightly wiser burden-bearer returned to the fray months later, committed to the use of levers and lifting devices, instead of brute force. These techniques did not save further mishap. A dishwasher under repair fell off the work surface and damaged a foot. The appliance still goes well, but the foot has never been the same. An amplifier, hurled on to the table in exasperation after a failed attempt at repair, landed on the other slippered foot. The amplifier worked for the first time when picked up, the foot matched its disabled neighbour.

High ladders and house painting always brought downfall and one unfortunate event brought a three litre can of paint cascading down 6 vertical metres to spray the immediate environment. I had been painting the apex of the soffit under the eaves, perched on the top rung of a long ladder. Initially, additional security was provided by a rope fixed on to a light-fitting on the house wall. Change of painting position to the other side of the doorway was more hazardous as there was no convenient security point.

The ladder seemed stable however. All seemed firm and secure, then the ladder moved. I clutched desperately at what had become an aerial steed. The ladder, with a will of its own, performed a parabolic arc while plunging to the ground. A desperate effort to restrain its fall, locked a hand under the ladder as it struck the ground. Struggling erect, from this catastrophe, I found my index finger sticking dramatically in fixed rigidity at right angles to the others. It had disarticulated! Hearing the crash, our eleven year old daughter arrived on the scene and with considerable aplomb announced.

"I know what to do daddy, you showed us when you were teaching us first aid." She grabbed the offending finger and yanked it straight.

I should have learned from these hazards of painting but later, in another paint incident, a de-ruster solution of ruddy hue splashed me liberally over eyes and face. At first sight of my bloody visage, an accident-conditioned wife, thought this accident was mortal. My house improving DIY days were finally decreed to be over.

A house call one afternoon saw me driving to a village idyllically snuggling between hillside and river. A haven for retirees, they took great pleasure from their gardens. There was healthy competition between villagers for the annual "Best garden" awards. Celia Rosenthal was active in the Gardener's club and an abundance of roses, flowers and well-kept lawns round her cottage were testimony to her pastoral efforts. She was seated with a foot up on the couch when I arrived to see her. A massive pad of cotton wool masked one foot.

" I put the gardening fork through my foot," she admitted wryly in explanation. A puncture wound identified the route the tine had taken. Although there was much bleeding, there was no extensive damage. I quickly applied pad and bandage and injected antibiotic and tetanus vaccine

"A few days off your feet and all should be well." I reassured her before departure. Driving back through the village I saw elderly residents trimming a tree, astride a wall clearing over- growth and laboring deep in ditches. These pastimes all seemed potential sources of trauma confirming my feeling that we saw much injury from bucolic leisure activities. I ruminated as I drove home on my own accident-prone gardening activities.

Gardening was always a challenge and I welcomed the introduction of powered gardening aids with scant regard to safety precautions. The end of a finger went in the hedge-trimmer and a toe was victim to a carelessly handled rotary grass mower. A long line of Cupressis Leylandia conifers proved a constant threat to physical well-being. A necessary garden screen, they grew a lusty metre per year and needed constant trimming, a task ever harder as they grew skyward. Five metres up in their branches, I cunningly built a walkway from old joists. Their linear junctions unfortunately parted a little over the years, leaving a gap to trap the unwary. Lower branches often hid these dangerous waypoints from view and I would inch along the wood-way wielding big loppers. Forgetful of the gap, once I injudiciously stepped out on to thin air! A nasty plunge to the ground with injury should have ensued but, still grasping the loppers, I made a graceful, controlled descent to land fairy-like on my feet, bemused at the abrupt change in status. There had been just sufficient leafy branches en route to slow the descent!

Disposal of clipped greenery was an eternal problem. Over time I built up a bank of decaying branches under the trees and a mountain of discarded material at one end of the line. During one dry summer, deciding to clear some of this debris, I calculated that a controlled fire would solve the problem and carefully ran out the garden hose to its full length, to control any over - exuberance of the intended conflagration. The hose did not quite reach the site, but undeterred, I set a match to the dried undergrowth.

Speedily the desiccated branches burst into flame and spread rapidly towards the adjacent trees. I belatedly realised they ran towards wooden sheds on neighbouring property, a few metres distant. I turned on the water to restrain the flames and found the stream did not quite reach the heart of what had rapidly become an inferno of flame, with smoke leaping high into the air. Leaves on the nearest standing trees were being scorched and toasted as I fought for control. A neighbour - fortuitously a fireman-came to my aid, just as the mini-firestorm threatened to engulf surroundings. Concerned for the safety of his property, his high-power garden hose drenched the flames. Mercifully the fire died down, but acrid smoke continued to pour from the heart of the blaze. Unbeknown to me, several layers of chipboard buried in the pile had resisted dampening down. They smouldered on for hours attracting the attention of the neighbourhood to my fecklessness. A healthy respect for fire was one lesson I took to heart.

Post traumatic headaches, an aversion to ladders, phobia for heights and sundry anatomical and psychological scars have made us wary of further DIY. Emancipated at last from self-inflicted Do it Yourself serfdom, I belatedly recognised that those who sentence themselves to such slavery are likely to meet a premature end upon the scaffold.

Happy Ending

Adele McDuff slipped into her seat and offered me a quiet,

"Good morning." I knew her to be a very pleasant lady of shy disposition and reticent of speech. Golden-skinned, there was a hint of eastern blood in her genetic past. She had the sensuous lines of face and lustrous eyes often associated with ladies of the Indian sub-continent. She never over-ran her consultation time, was always courteous, but I always seemed to have to drag information from her. Her conversation was brief, almost terse, and to the point.

"I am sorry to be troubling you Doctor." She always started the interview with an apology for taking up my time. She seemed to guard her thoughts carefully. Over several years of professional contact, I still had only a superficial awareness of her real 'self' and what made her tick. There seemed to be hidden depths to her personality which I was not allowed to explore.

She rarely visited with a personal complaint and her interest was primarily in her two children. Married to a taxi-driver, she was the business head in the partnership. She had married very young and had a pregnancy when nineteen years old. In the days before ultra-sound scans, diagnosing multiple pregnancies was not always easy and we were all surprised when twins arrived.

I recalled my follow-up obstetric home visit at this time. Mrs. Lofty the maternal grandmother arrived on an apparently rare visit to her daughter. She bestowed a few ungracious words on Adele who was fatigued after a prolonged delivery, gave a passing glance at the babies and left in haste. She seemed to have no interest in Adele and less in the grandchildren, an unusual response to the safe arrival of new-borns. Immaculately dressed and bejewelled she was a supercilious individual, with an exaggerated sense of social station and self importance. Married to a senior civil servant in the Indian Colonial service, she had become accustomed to a retinue of servants and had conveniently forgotten her own humble upbringing.

Her own mother had been a bar-maid in a Glasgow public-house and daughter Gwen had escaped her humble tenement upbringing by marrying a young lad on the first step in a Civil Service career. He had been posted abroad and made a rapid advance up the promotion ladder. The Lofty's had lived for some time in Sri Lanka - then Ceylon - and had acquired status as colonial whites. The unpleasant attributes of snobbery and aloofness acquired abroad had been retained on their final return home to Britain. Adele had introduced me to her mother. Her response left me with the impression she believed she was dealing with an underling. Her reluctant hand-shake reminded me of the transient grasp on a slippery, dying fish caught when fishing, as she released fingers quickly from the encounter.

In time to come, Adele struggled with heavy demands from the babies, made routine vaccination visits to the surgery and never complained of her stressful existence. Unfortunately, as the children grew up, behavioural problems suggested that they had autism. with Geordie the little boy severely impaired. Jemina his sister, was diagnosed as having Attention Deficit Syndrome and her learning was slow. They were both in these days classified as retarded and were a great trial to Adele and Ben.

"I really do not know what to do with them". Adele confessed on one visit after they had both fallen from a garden tree and had skin gashes which needed stitching. Neither seemed to have any sense of fear and dared each other to embark on dangerous exploits. I had seen them once hanging outside the window frame of an upstairs window, when passing in the car. Both children had temper tantrums and needed constant surveillance. Their harum-scarum behavioural exploits began to be the talk of the village. In due course they went off to school and Ben's taxis came in handy for the school runs.

Teachers were no more able than Adele with the recalcitrant pair and they were passed to "special needs" colleagues for one to one tuition. Their short attention span limited the value of special schooling, but they were retained in the conventional classroom when Geordie threatened the teacher with a knife, social workers became involved. He ultimately became so anti-social and aggressive that he was placed in permanent social care establishment. On his rare home vacations he complained that Adele was physically abusing him. This brought unfounded suspicion from social workers.

I was called to testify by a truculent social worker.

"He is being physically abused," she stated definitively pointing out bruises on his body which I thought had an accidental cause. The MacDuff's had to submit to a legal investigation. There was no support for his accusations and I verified that they had in my opinion always been upright citizens and exemplary parents. This was very stressful time for both. Despite evidence to the contrary, visitations to their son were curtailed and supervised, a situation which ultimately resulted in their isolation from the youth. Fostered on several occasions his dangerous, unreliable behaviour finally had the authorities recognise he was a hazard in the community and he was permanently institutionalised.

Jemina reached her teens and her promiscuous behaviour brought intervention by the police.. She was an easy conquest for village lads and Adele and Ben were relieved when she attracted the attentions of Jim a kindly, simple minded, refuse collection man. The pair became inseparable and married. The baby dauchter arrived six months later and Adele found she had another off-spring to rear, as neither Jemina, or her husband were up to the demands of parenthood. The new-born had spina bifida, a congenital spinal condition and would always be physically disabled and require careful nursing and nurturing.

I began to see Adele, Jemina and baby more frequently. Austin the baby failed to thrive. Health visitors were concerned that his mum was attempting to wean him directly on to fish and chips! Jemina struggled ineffectually to maintain husband and baby. She became obese and slovenly and her husband took up with a slim and more attractive nurse.

The call came at 2 am. from Adele.

"Its Jemina she is in bed and not breathing properly." Grabbing the emergency bag, I raced to her house to be met by Adele,

"I am so sorry to disturb you doctor, but I cannot waken Jemina." I rushed upstairs to the bed room to find her dead in bed. A used pack of sleeping pills and a half full bottle of whisky sat on the bedside table. Adele, pale white and stony-faced, but dry-eyed stood beside me.

"She found out today that Jim was cheating on her." Adele offered. "I did not know she had these pills and she never ever drank spirits. I did not think it would come to this." I organised a post mortem, which later confirmed suicide, and ought to console Adele, who showed no overt signs of distress.

"I am fine doctor. I am worried about Austin. Jim has been living away and the baby is alone." Then determinedly, "I shall take him home." She devoted herself to the baby's care and his physical condition improved and I rarely saw her.

It was Ben who consulted me next.

"I am passing blood in the water." he announced and fearing a nasty underlying cause, I fixed early investigation of his symptoms. He was diagnosed as having a malignant cancer of the prostate gland. Many men suffer from cancer of this organ and most live a long time after diagnosis and die from other causes. Ben had a very aggressive tumour, which had possibly spread to other body parts.

The immediate future was going to be difficult for both. Not for the first time I quizzed Adele her about family support. Her response had always been a rebuff. This time however,

"Ben's parents are dead and I never see mine." She blurted out soulfully, "My mother has rarely seen my children and has yet to see Austin.

I was dismayed at this revelation. Poor Adele had largely coped on her own with a son suffering from Asperger's Syndrome who had died in a mental institution and a hyperactive and not mentally bright daughter who had now died prematurely. To these tragedies, had now been added, a physically-disabled grandson and Ben's supportive care. I reached for the tissues assuming another appointment schedule was about to be wrecked. This was not the time for a truncated consultation. The opportunity to break through the barrier of reserve and cast light on her social and psychological state did not occur. She pulled herself together and stoically reverted to type.

Some months went by, but then she started consulting for minor problems relating to grandson and self and I tried to explore her feelings to no avail. She arrived one day complaining of deafness and I reached for the auroscope to examine her ears. There was some wax in the ear canals and I prescribed some wax-softening drops for her to use until a repeat appointment.Then I would syringe the canals and free them from waxy obstacles to her hearing.

She returned a week later for ear syringing; now the province of the practice nurse but then carried out by the doctor. The procedure did allow time to chat with the patient, but I was running late in the surgery session and rather peremptorily dealt with the chore in an effort to catch up. The ear cleansing process completed, the inevitable occurred. She stood in the doorway about to leave then turned to say,

"While I am here Doctor."

Conditioned to these words, so often repeated by patients about to expose the real reason for their visit and time-pressured, I inadvertently revealed sympathetic feelings and torpedoed another consultation time-schedule.

"What a terrible load you carry. Life has been unkind to you. Tell me about it," I encouraged and a pent-up flood of long-blocked emotions finally engulfed her. Suddenly the constraint of years was gone and she burst into a torrent of tears.

"It's endless," she wailed "and I can't speak about the half of it. They never wanted me." She sobbed, "Never ever! They sent me to boarding school when I was four and left me on my own in England while they were in Ceylon. I was in many different schools before I was sixteen and they rarely came to see me. Sometimes I was left at the end of term with no one to collect me. It was terrible and I felt so alone. When they came home to London to stay for good, I was still left in boarding school. No one wanted me."

Slowly her neglected childhood came to light. It seemed that she had arrived as an unwanted pregnancy and I wondered if she had been an illegitimate product of a love affair between mother and Asian. Illegitimate children were not uncommon among expatriates, but affairs were usually hushed up. Abortions were then very dangerous and many conceptions were unhappily carried to term, the child was presented and brought up as a legitimate offspring. Absorbed into the family, many enjoyed a privileged childhood. In this instance the parents had met some of their obligations, but distanced themselves from Adele thrusting her into a lonely solitary traumatising existence. It seemed remarkable that she had maintained contact with them on maturity. She had struggled to maintain a relationship with an uncaring mother.

Gradually the sobbing subsided and she apologised for her emotional breakdown.

"I have never told anyone else about this before, not even Ben, but I feel better for sharing it now. Thank you for your time and patience," as she reverted to her retiring self.

"I suggest you come back for a longer appointment and we can talk this through a bit more" I offered, and she willingly agreed to return for a longer consultation.

While checking the daily mail after her visit I was dismayed to read a letter from the urologist regarding Ben's condition. "Aggressive cancer, which has spread beyond the prostate to other organs. Outlook very poor", the report read. Only palliative treatment was possible and they believed that he had only months to live. Adele's burden of care was now an overload and I wondered how she would cope with this additional disaster. I arranged for both to come to her extended appointment visit. They took the bad news stoically and I asked how they would manage with baby and Ben's failing health.

Independent as ever, Adele assured me. "We will manage." and disdained an offer of social support. Ben declined physically very quickly and Adele refused help from support services until near his end. Her name was added to the visit list one morning. When I arrived she announced dry eyed-that Ben had died. She had scant family support to deal with her grief, but focussed her attention once again on her grandson. He was slow in learning to walk and I wondered whether he would ever be able become mobile and care for himself.

She called in to the surgery when he developed an itchy rash and revealed that her father now in his eighties had died. Her mother had made belated contact when Adele had made a special visit the family home in England. She was dismayed to find that Mrs Lofty had early Alzheimer's disease and was not coping well at home. She lived in a palatial villa in Southsea, a four hour single journey from the Borders, which Adele began to make once a week. She felt obligated to her mother's care although she received scant appreciation for her journeys.

"She doesn't always know me and is very argumentative when I visit and tells me to go away and leave her," Adele remarked.

"It's a trying time for you and a long journey each week." I commented.

"Yes, but she is my mother and I will do it as long as she needs me." she replied.

The old lady deteriorated slowly over the next two years. She rarely had a good word for her daughter and did not acknowledge any grandchildren. She was transferred to a care home and Adele continued to visit regularly. Latterly her mother no longer recognised her.

I was now very concerned about Adele's health. She was pale and distressed when I saw her and had become very agitated.

"I feel very low and cannot sleep." She said despondently. "Money is tight and I can barely make ends meet." When her husband had died they had been close to bankruptcy. I mused that her mother's demise would surely bring an inheritance to free her from financial worries. Mrs Lofty now in her eighties clung on to life in the protected cocoon of the care home with savings gradually being drained away by care fees. I felt Adele had clinical depression and prescribed anti-depressive medication.

Then Joe my partner rang to advise me of a home visit he had made the previous evening.

"I had to call on the McDuffs. The wee one had a headache and was off colour. He had a fever and a fine shin rash and I wasn't sure if the headache was due to the spina bifida or an infection. He also had a fine pink skin rash and I wondered about meningitis and sent him to the infirmary."

The cause unfortunately proved to be meningitis, a death-threatening condition which did not respond to the limited treatment then available. He died within days, leaving Adele absolutely distraught. She had always presented a stoic acceptance of all the many adversities that had come her way over the years, but this proved to be the last straw. Within days of this tragic bereavement her mother died and she was relieved of that burden of care, she was left with no familial support whatsoever in her own time of need. She went into an intense depression and became suicidal.

"I might as well do away with myself" she blurted out. "Life has nothing for me" and realistically I could empathise with her emotions.

Psychologically-abused by parents, mother of mentally-disabled children, a loving husband lost in his prime and then the grandson - her raison d'etre - had died prematurely. She could only reflect on a life of unmitigated misfortune. She became a very regular surgery visitor as I monitored the medication, which took some weeks to become effective. Over a few months she improved mentally and almost in rebound visited with a request for travel vaccinations.

"I have come into some money Doctor, from Mum's will and I have decided to do some of the things I have always wanted to do, I am going off on a world cruise." I had some misgivings about this plan, as a cruise ship can be a lonely place for single travellers and I was concerned that her depression would return. My worries were misplaced however.

Six months passed before Adele made a final visit. She was smartly dressed in the height of fashion, at odds with her usual quiet wearing apparel. Her expression exuded well-being and her face was radiant. Rather coyly she responded to my,

"How was the cruise?"

"Oh, it was wonderful," and then rather shyly, "I met a gentleman on board and we found we had much in common." Then after a pause, "He is a widower and we got on very well together. In fact he asked me to marry him." A further pause and then hesitantly, as if she was seeking my approval, "I said Yes and we are getting married in a month. I am going to live with him in India."

“Well that is good news.” I responded and we chatted for a few minutes before she made her departure. The gentleman was a newspaper proprietor. By a quirk of fate Adele was returning to a life of affluence on the continent of her birth. A lifetime of tragedy and exclusion had been reversed and a happier future seemed assured. I wished her well and she emigrated shortly afterwards.

Several years later I was attending a medical conference in Delhi. When passing through the crowded hotel foyer, I bumped into an elegant lady chatting to a distinguished-looking Indian businessman. She turned towards me as I apologised.

“Why Doctor fancy seeing you here. How are you?” Taken aback and plumbing my memory bank, I finally faltered,

“Adele?”

“Yes. I am pleased to see you. May I introduce my husband?”

They insisted on a lunch together. He proved a charming man who obviously cared deeply for his new wife. The encounter had me reflect on the strange vicissitudes of life. Adele had gone from an unhappy, unwanted existence through a series of devastating misfortunes, to a loving environment in the location of her birth.

Epilogue

Thirty five years after arriving in Harborough I wrote my last prescription, closed the medical-bag and said goodbye to the last patient. The intervening years had brought joy and fulfilment, heartache and sorrow. For better or worse, I had cared for the local community and seen many changes in health care. People were healthier, lived longer and were more affluent. Infectious diseases had largely been mastered and babies and mothers now rarely died at child birth. Household and workplace trauma had declined.

A handful of medications had been replaced with a large compendium of medicines and a few antibiotics by many. Simple x-rays had been overtaken by computerised scans, extensive invasive surgery by key-hole techniques, primitive ultra-sound by echo-cardiography. Genetic engineering and organ replacement was routine.

Psychological rather than physical ailments now dominated GP surgery consultations. House visitation had become infrequent and family doctors worked conventional hours, were never disturbed at night and had weekends to recuperate from work-demands. Financially secure, with optimal work conditions, they should have been content but, burdened with bureaucracy, many had become unhappy with their lot and sought early retirement.

In retrospect, my consulting years may have seen the NHS family doctor providing a service that was personalised, accessible and immediate - a model which may never return. Patients were privileged, but neither they nor politicians could appreciate the value of the service provided until it was lost. My departure coincided with the end of an era.

Twenty years after I had left medical practice, I met a couple of patients not seen in the interim. The husband, formerly a local policeman, had retired and grandchildren were now on the scene. After a few reminiscences his wife said,

"We still think of ourselves as being your patients, after all these years. You were always there when we needed you." a tribute and fitting end perhaps to the story of the life of a family doctor working in the last decades of the 20th century.

ND - #0255 - 080726 - C0 - 210/148/11 - PB - 9781784564223 - Gloss Lamination